DATE DUE			
MR 30 '74 MR 2 8			
MR 30 '74			
Staff			
MY 27 '73			
FE 19 74			
JY 30 '74			
MAR 1 5 1975			
MAY 2 3 1984			
FEB 17 1985			
APR 1 7 1987			
MAR 2 8 1988			
JAN 2 9 1991			
JUL 3 1 1992			
FEB 2 0 1995			
FEB 2 4 RET'D			
GAYLORD			PRINTED IN U.S.A.

TWENTIETH CENTURY INTERPRETATIONS
OF
WOMEN IN LOVE

A Collection of Critical Essays

Edited by

STEPHEN J. MIKO

Prentice-Hall, Inc.  *Englewood Cliffs, N. J.*

THE COLLEGE AND SEMINARY LIBRARY
NAPERVILLE, ILLINOIS

Quotations from *Women in Love* by D. H. Lawrence, copyright 1920, 1922 by David Herbert Lawrence, renewed 1948, 1950 by Frieda Lawrence are reprinted by permission of The Viking Press, Inc., Laurence Pollinger Ltd., and the Estate of Frieda Lawrence. Quotations from *The Collected Letters of D. H. Lawrence,* edited by Harry T. Moore, copyright © 1962 by Angelo Ravagli and C. Montague Weekley, Executors of the Estate of Frieda Lawrence Ravagli; 1932 by The Estate of D. H. Lawrence and 1934 by Frieda Lawrence; © 1933, 1948, 1953, 1954 and each year 1956–1962 by Angelo Ravagli and C. Montague Weekley, Executors of the Estate of Frieda Lawrence Ravagli. All rights reserved. Reprinted by permission of The Viking Press, Inc., Laurence Pollinger Ltd., and the Estate of Frieda Lawrence.

Copyright © 1969 by Prentice-Hall, Inc., Englewood Cliffs, New Jersey. A SPECTRUM BOOK. All rights reserved. No part of this book may be reproduced in any form or by any means without permission in writing from the publisher. C–13-962431-7; P–13-962423-6. *Library of Congress Catalog Card Number 70–96966.* Printed in the United States of America.

Current printing (last number):
10 9 8 7 6 5 4 3 2 1

PRENTICE-HALL INTERNATIONAL, INC. (*London*)
PRENTICE-HALL OF AUSTRALIA, PTY. LTD. (*Sydney*)
PRENTICE-HALL OF CANADA, LTD. (*Toronto*)
PRENTICE-HALL OF INDIA PRIVATE LIMITED (*New Delhi*)
PRENTICE-HALL OF JAPAN, INC. (*Tokyo*)

A Note on References

Unless otherwise indicated, all references to *Women In Love* are to the Phoenix edition (London: William Heinemann, Ltd., 1954), which is paginated identically with the Viking Compass edition.

Contents

Introduction, *by Stephen J. Miko* — 1

Part One—*Interpretations*

Dies Irae, *by George H. Ford* — 20

Suspended Form: Lawrence's Theory of Fiction in *Women in Love*, *by Alan Friedman* — 40

Women in Love and the Lawrencean Aesthetic, *by David J. Gordon* — 50

The Discovery of Form, *by Julian Moynahan* — 61

No Man's Land, *by Mark Spilka* — 73

The Substance of *Women in Love*, *by Eliseo Vivas* — 85

Part Two—*View Points*

Robert B. Heilman — 97
Edwin Honig — 103
Leone Vivante — 105
Daniel A. Weiss — 111

Chronology of Important Dates — 115
Notes on the Editor and Contributors — 117
Selected Bibliography — 119

Introduction

by Stephen J. Miko

I

Lawrence's completion of *Women in Love* brought a tentative and even discouraged note to his letters.

> There is another novel, sequel to *The Rainbow*, called *Women in Love*. I don't know if Huebsch has got the MS. yet. I don't think anybody will publish this, either. This actually does contain the results in one's soul of the war: it is purely destructive, not like *The Rainbow*, destructive-consummating. It is very wonderful and terrifying, even to me who have written it. I have hardly read it again. I suppose, however, it will be a long time without being printed—if ever it is printed.[1]

This was written July 27, 1917. The book was finally published in November, 1920, but in a foreign land (the United States) and in a limited edition for subscribers only. In May, 1921 it appeared in England, pursued by threats of libel. Some minor changes were made, the threats quieted down, and Lawrence's fifth novel was somewhat precariously sent forth to a British public who in 1915 had brought about the suppression of *The Rainbow* as pornography (one reviewer called it an "orgy of sexiness"). This suppression was, in fact, the main reason that *Women in Love,* essentially finished in the fall of 1916, took four years to find a publisher. But this is only one of a number of reasons why Lawrence showed little optimism in 1917.

Although the suppression of *The Rainbow* in England (it was published, but only with some cutting of the "pornographic" passages, by Huebsch in the United States) was unquestionably the major blow of Lawrence's literary career, it was only one of a series of disappointments and disillusionments which afflicted him during the years of the First World War. Unlike many of his contemporaries, he regarded the war from the first as a disaster: "The War finished me: it was

---

[1] Letter to Waldo Frank, July 27, 1917. From Harry T. Moore's *The Collected Letters of D. H. Lawrence* (New York: The Viking Press, Inc., 1962), I, 519. Hereafter *Letters*.

the spear through the side of all sorrows and hopes."[2] Throughout the whole period of the war, which he spent in England, his letters show a growing despair and disgust over the useless slaughter, especially when the death notices of friends and acquaintances (Rupert Brooke, and Katherine Mansfield's brother Leslie) began to arrive. Never susceptible to national enthusiasms, Lawrence had no sympathy with the detestation of the "Huns" fostered by British and American propaganda. To make matters more difficult, he was married to a German of baronial descent, whose distant cousin, Manfred von Richthofen, became the most famous of the German flyers. Frieda Lawrence made no pretense of loving England more than Germany; she corresponded regularly with her family; and she sang German songs, even during a blackout. In this signing Lawrence joined, half in defiance of already snooping authority, half from a sheer love of fun. His reward was repeated searching of his cottage in Cornwall, abuse from neighbors as well as officials, and eviction in October, 1917, with orders to report his whereabouts regularly to the police.

Lawrence's response to this persecution was so incredulous as to be called "ingenuous" by one of his biographers.[3] "I cannot even conceive how I have incurred suspicion—have not the faintest notion. We are as innocent even of pacifist activities, let alone spying of any sort, as the rabbits in the field outside."[4] Yet beneath this ingenuousness lies a hope, even an optimism, that must be understood if we are to understand passages like this one:

> I've got again into one of those horrible sleeps from which I can't wake. I can't brush it aside to wake up. You know those horrible sleeps when one is struggling to wake up and can't? I was like it all autumn—and now I am again like it. Everything has a touch of delirium, even the apple-blossom. And when I see a snake winding rapidly in the marshy places, I think I am mad.[5]

"Madness" is a word Lawrence used often to refer to the war and its effects. Although this passage was written in 1915, shortly after the war began, Lawrence's willingness to see the whole of civilization as mad and impossible seems to have been permanently increased by the expulsion from Cornwall. Frieda claimed that "something changed in Lawrence forever." But if it did, some other, more positive attitudes were present before. The recognition of madness presupposes some

---

[2] ? January 31, 1915. *Letters*, I, 309. At this time the war was less than three months old.
[3] Harry T. Moore, *The Intelligent Heart* (New York: Grove Press, 1962), p. 297.
[4] *Letters*, I, 527.
[5] *Ibid.*, I, 339.

standard of sanity, just as incredulousness presupposes belief. By similar thinking the extent to which a book is "purely destructive" can only be measured by an understanding of what is being destroyed. We may seek such understanding by looking briefly at Lawrence's life before the war.

II

By the time Lawrence finished *Women in Love* he was over thirty—still young, but with four novels, a book of short stories, a series of essays, and a book of poems already published. In 1916 a travel book and a second book of poems came out, and in the space before the publication of *Women in Love* a series of philosophic and critical works, a book of history, more poems, and another novel were completed. There was little doubt in literary circles that Lawrence was by 1916 one of the most significant, as well as one of the most versatile, writers of the time. Some called him a genius from the time of his first publication, though it was difficult then (and still is now) to say just what sort of genius he was. He did not himself make much of this term; it is pleasantly absent from his letters. But he clearly thought of himself as a writer of unusual gifts and unusual purpose.

To be accurate about Lawrence's purpose is not easy. The words "prophetic," "visionary," "religious," frequently applied to Lawrence and his writings, give some indication of the difficulties. Some notion of purpose is implicit in them all, but semantic analysis will not take us very far. At least all imply a search for meaning beyond that of the logical positivist: a search that extends toward what anthropologists call "basic" or "primitive" activities: man's attempts to relate himself to the forces that govern the universe, whatever they may be. So Lawrence has also been called a primitive, a myth-maker, a seeker of dark gods. His detractors have accused him of stupid emotionalism, obsession with sex, anti-intellectualism; his supporters say he was truer to feeling than reason can be, treated sex as a religious activity, denied the mind its right to inhibit. To sort out these differences takes a book (a good number have been written), but at least they all imply a quest for meaning of unusual intensity and inclusiveness. This quest emerged gradually, from hesitant literary efforts and, more fundamentally, a troubled childhood.

Lawrence began writing poems and stories in his late teens. He was not confident of his abilities. "And I remember the slightly self-conscious Sunday afternoon, when I was nineteen, and I 'composed' my first two 'poems.' One was to *Guelder-Roses,* and one was to *Campions,* and most young ladies would have done better: at least I hope so."[6] The poems do not refute him, though some written not much later were impressive enough to interest Ford Madox Hueffer (later Ford Madox Ford), editor of the new *English Review*.[7] It was Hueffer who "discovered" Lawrence and introduced him to the London literary world. Thanks to this introduction Lawrence found it easy to get his first novel, *The White Peacock*, published. But none of this took place until Lawrence was twenty-four, and even then it was only through the agency of Jessie Chambers, his first love, that his poems reached *The English Review*. The five-year gap indicates, among other things, considerable sensitivity and fear of failure. Even though he had won a short-story prize while at college, he had also had a poem rejected by the college paper, and his one attempt to seek encouragement from a professional writer had resulted in the return of his manuscript unread.

All young writers are self-conscious. But Lawrence had perhaps more reasons than most. Born in 1885 to a barely literate midland miner and a literate but strict minister's daughter, he spent his childhood and youth conscious of the threat of poverty. Great bitterness would arise when his father drank up any of the family income. His mother was an abstainer all her life, and she worked successfully to instill in her children a contempt for moral inconsistency and irresponsibility. She was ambitious, especially eager that they avoid "going into the pit" with their father. Here, too, she was successful; none of her three sons was a miner, Lawrence least of all. He was the youngest boy, closer to his two sisters than to his brothers. He was frail and even sickly, particularly susceptible to chest colds, which finally developed into tuberculosis and killed him at forty-four.

Lawrence's continual bad health contributed both to his preference for female company and to a tendency to rely upon imagination rather than act. He developed a particular sensitivity to emotional turmoil, which, though a great asset to a novelist, caused considerable torture to a young boy. Because his mother early won him over against his father, he observed their regular conflicts as a partisan. The security of taking sides may have been better than utter bewilderment, but his bond with his mother became so strong that only her death made mar-

[6] From Lawrence's "Foreword" to his *Collected Poems*, published 1928. Reprinted in *The Complete Poems of D. H. Lawrence*, ed. Vivian de Sola Pinto and Warren Roberts (New York: The Viking Press, Inc., 1964).

[7] By his own account, which doesn't quite square with the facts of publication, Hueffer was even more impressed by the early story "Odour of Chrysanthemums," which induced him to announce the new genius. See Harry Moore's *Intelligent Heart*, p. 125. Edward Nehls reprints the passage from Hueffer's *Parade's End* in his *D. H. Lawrence: Composite Biography* (Madison: University of Wisconsin Press, 1957), I, 106.

riage possible. With the death of his elder brother in 1901 (Lawrence was sixteen), a peculiarly intense form of mutual dependence seems to have set in. By the time Mrs. Lawrence died in 1910, Lawrence had wrecked his first love and found himself incapable of forming a second. It was not at all clear then that even her death would free him.

Most of this is faithfully recorded in Lawrence's third novel, *Sons and Lovers* (1913), in which he claimed he "shed his sickness"—meaning his excessive attachment to his mother. But he did not shed either his sensitivity or his self-consciousness. Throughout his life he was an exile, a seeker of pastoral havens, which he endeavored—mostly without success—to populate with his closest friends. He had difficulty keeping friends, not in making them. Apparently he was too demanding: too ready to criticize, too direct in anger, too willing to transform people into unflattering characters in his novels. He seemed to seek some unconditional bond which would fortify friendship against all such attacks and even allow retaliation in kind. All of these tendencies are related to his childhood. The man who could be virulent with intimates is also the young man who is too fearful to risk his poems, and both are the boy who agonizes yet exults when his mother excoriates his father. To put it very simply, Lawrence's sensitivity led him to demand more from family, friends, and even "the world" than most of us, growing up under circumstances where cynicism is easier than idealism, are likely to expect. Lawrence's demands shaped both his life and his art; the form they took was importantly determined by both of his parents.

It is easy to connect Lawrence's demands on life to his mother's ambition for him. He was encouraged at a very early age to rise above his station: he read voluminously; he won scholarships; he studied to be a teacher. But to his mother success meant largely material success, or success in the eyes of the world. When it became obvious that Lawrence was more interested in painting and reading than in business—his elder brother had been getting on very well in business when he suddenly died—there was disappointment. Lawrence complained that she didn't care about the quality of his achievements at all, only about their success. Jessie Chambers, however, cared a good deal. She is the figure upon whom Miriam in *Sons and Lovers* is based, and her account of Lawrence's adolescence is, after that novel, the best one we have.[8] She portrays Lawrence as a passionately intense, intellectual, lively boy, with a gift for bringing joy to others, and especially for making them "see." Both Jessie and his mother encouraged these gifts, but they encouraged differently. Mrs. Lawrence

---

[8] *D. H. Lawrence: A Personal Record* (New York: Barnes & Noble, Inc., 1965 [originally published in 1935]).

loved her son and believed in his ability, but Jessie was willing to call him an artist.

Both mother and sweetheart, then, helped to give direction to the artist as a young man. He wanted most to succeed to please his mother; he wanted almost as badly to find form for the pressure inside him, a vitality which seemed to include adolescent sexuality, love of painting and literature, love of nature, an urge to write—all of these mixed up, impossible to separate out. What was worse, some of these loves seemed to exclude others; not only were both his mother and Jessie seeking to possess him directly, but the need for success led to practical activity and the need for self-expression quite another way—a way much less clear. So Lawrence gave in for a while to the former; he taught school for four years in Croyden, south of London. But he didn't like teaching young boys much, and he wrote his first novel in the evenings.

All this helps to account for Lawrence's persistent touchiness; the pattern of conflict briefly sketched here was never completely resolved. Although he became surer of himself as he grew older, he was not capable of the sort of acceptance of his lot which would allow him to work, say, in a bank during the day and write poems at night. Part of his tendency to alienate his intimates was surely fear that they would betray him, would not understand and love him without conditions. Jessie had conditions; his mother had conditions; he had to struggle particularly hard to find his own way. It is from this struggle, I think, that much of his intensity derives. But to get even a meager understanding of the directions it takes we need also to consider his father.

Lawrence tried for quite a while to ignore his father, but he finally came to recognize that this was impossible. Lawrence admitted that he had treated his father unfairly in *Sons and Lovers*; he meant, presumably, that the scenes of Walter Morel's drunkenness and surliness, based on Arthur Lawrence's drunkenness and surliness, left out too much of what was good in Arthur Lawrence. But recent critics have disputed Lawrence's judgment of his own book, I think with good reason. The "good side" of Arthur Lawrence is there too, only a bit submerged. Dorothy Van Ghent has even argued that the real values of *Sons and Lovers* are those associated with Walter Morel: especially an untrammeled, free, vital response to the world.[9] Although the force of these values is clear only by hindsight—they were certainly unclear to the Lawrence who wrote in 1911—there can be no doubt that

---

[9] *The English Novel: Form and Function* (New York: Holt, Rinehart & Winston, Inc., 1953). Other critics who make important use of this shift in Lawrence's attitude are George Ford in his *Double Measure* (New York: Holt, Rinehart & Winston, Inc., 1965) and H. M. Daleski in his *The Forked Flame* (Evanston: Northwestern University Press, 1965).

Lawrence accepted more from his father than he realized in his youth. And, as it turns out, his father, the miners before mechanization of the mines, and other rough and vital types (most notoriously, gamekeepers) consistently represent for Lawrence the freedom his mother would not give him.

The need for this freedom became clearer with age; although it had not much effect on Lawrence's relations with his actual father, it certainly influenced Lawrence's conception of his purpose. To his mother's moral force and basic consistency he tried to add his father's freer, more directly expressive vitality. In short, he became something of a vitalist, inventing a morality, a psychology, and even a metaphysics through which he tried to retain his mother's essential seriousness as well as his father's ability for uninhibited, hedonistic response. Obviously this was not an easy task, and it is only with a string of qualifications that he can be said to have succeeded. But the intensity of his purpose is at least partly explained by the urgency of these opposed values in his childhood; Lawrence had to make sense out of them to survive.

III

When Lawrence began to write, his talent was most evident in his descriptions of nature; he began to record and develop what was already a skill in conversation. Although he did not altogether avoid a romantic prettiness and a gratuitous gloom (critics point to the influence of Thomas Hardy), Hueffer and others immediately recognized a directness and freshness of response—perhaps the one point on which most critics of Lawrence, admirers as well as detractors, agree. But as Lawrence continued to write, he began to relate, or at least try to relate, the various ingredients in his adolescent conflicts. In *The White Peacock* two virile men, a farmer and a gamekeeper, both turn out to be doomed. We find also possessive and dominant women, toward whom the attitude of the narrator is ambivalent. The narrator himself is significantly without much force or personality, though he is vaguely presented as an intellectual. He is also rather effeminate, displaying homosexual yearnings as well as envy of motherhood. It is in fact only in natural description that a fairly consistent attitude of acceptance and enjoyment prevails, and even to this there are exceptions; gloom lingers even here.

The problems implicit in *The White Peacock* are the problems with which Lawrence struggled throughout his life and which are most nearly resolved in *The Rainbow* and *Women in Love*. The two doomed virile males are both connected with the land. The gamekeeper must die because he has rejected all the usual social and cultural ties for an almost feral existence; the farmer degenerates into alcoholism partly because he leaves the land to go in for horse-trading and socialism, partly because he is mysteriously inadequate before a more sophisticated "cultured" woman. In these two figures we can see an attempt to affirm a free pastoral existence, but an inability to do so because of an important yearning for social and cultural achievement. As Lawrence's thought developed, the former became much more important than the latter (which is seen in *Women in Love* largely as inhibitory), but we must not forget that he was a novelist and an intellectual, and so is Birkin an intellectual. Birkin, in fact, is clearly a more mature version of Cyril, the narrator of *The White Peacock*; both display ambivalence toward women as mothers and lovers, and both seek male friendship which has a physical dimension (whether or not this is "homosexual," or what we mean if we call it so, is discussed below: see the essays by Spilka and Ford). The most important difference between them is that Birkin "comes through," while Cyril does not. The fact that he does indicates that Lawrence has at least partially resolved his problems with women.

This resolution took at least two more novels, his mother's death, and his stealing of another man's wife to accomplish. Lawrence's second novel, *The Trespasser,* is one of his least known, probably for good reasons. The book is mostly devoted to a passionate and tortured holiday on the Isle of Wight, stolen by a married musician and his female student. Although again it contains good description, and even convincing moments of passion, it is inferior to *The White Peacock* because of a persistent, almost Wagnerian *weltschmerz;* everything is mysteriously and unconvincingly doomed from the start, culminating in the powerfully portrayed suicide of the man. The man, like the men in the first novel, is weak; he can't seem to cope with his belligerent wife, his swarming family, or his new and overwhelming love. He keeps thinking his failures are connected with a mysterious fatality in nature, and the love scenes themselves reach out to "connect" with nature, foreshadowing a technique used much more successfully in *The Rainbow*. Here the moaning and sighing is often embarrassing, but beneath it we can perceive Lawrence working at his own problems: he was clearly reaching for some way to relate erotic experience to "ultimates," and he sought these ultimates in his natural surroundings (his debt to the romantics must be acknowledged). If in *The White Peacock* he had difficulty relating virility to the social and cultural, here he concentrates on sexual experience itself. Both of these concerns appear importantly in *Women in Love*.

His third novel, *Sons and Lovers,* is vastly superior to his first two, because in it he finds the courage to write directly of his own life. In

Introduction 9

effect, he lives through his childhood again and tries, with considerable success, to make sense of it. He finally explores with fascinating thoroughness not only the events but the quality of his early life, and, though there is very little analytic commentary on his conflict with mother, father, and lovers, they are so convincingly lived through as to be—almost—resolved in the writing. In this book Lawrence demonstrates several crucial gains in his understanding of himself and of the world: most prominently, he recognizes very fully the nature of his attachment to his mother; he shows that it can be both blessing and bondage, creative of character but destructive of life. He also explores directly and offers, often implicitly, criticism of his own adolescent yearnings and uncertainties—not just those "derived" from his mother, but those which direct and express his urge for freedom and self-realization. He recognizes, perhaps only unconsciously, the importance of his father in this urge for freedom, and his very technique shows a willingness to explore objectively the complexity of human emotion, both that centered in his family and that which leads to rejection of the family. None of this results in finding final answers to the conflicting demands and needs of a young writer. But there is certainly some truth in Lawrence's claim that there he "shed his sickness." His next two novels support him.

The gloom that overbore all else in Lawrence's first two novels was largely missing in his third; still more so in *The Rainbow* (1915), his fourth. His letters show, in fact, a new sort of wonder at what he is producing. From the calm pronouncement that he is "writing away at a novel rather more cheerful than *Sons and Lovers*" he goes on to complain that his new work is "weird," that he has "no notion of what it [is] about." Yet it appears he does: "I can only write what I feel pretty strongly about; and that, at present, is the relation between men and women. After all, it is *the* problem of today, the establishment of a new relation, or the readjustment of the old one, between men and women." [10]

Here is one of Lawrence's central statements of his evolving purpose, which he is finally beginning to articulate in his published writings. The "relation . . . between men and women" is certainly the central concern of *The Rainbow,* and at this point in his life his very survival seemed to him bound up with it. In April, 1912, he had met Frieda von Richthofen Weekley, wife of a professor of literature at Nottingham; a month later he had run off with her to the continent, where he finished *Sons and Lovers* and began *The Rainbow*. Although it took two years to get a divorce from Frieda's husband, and although he and Frieda fought a lot, often violently, the new

[10] *Letters,* I, 200.

relation held. Of course it got into his writing, determining even the title of his third book of poems, *Look! We Have Come Through!* It also influenced his next two novels, especially *Women in Love,* parts of which were apparently written before what are now the early chapters of *The Rainbow.*

What Lawrence set out to write in the spring of 1913 was, curiously enough, a quick "pot boiler" for "jeunes filles" to be called "The Sisters." He soon found it necessary to put aside 200 pages of a more "serious" work because the pot boiler entranced and compelled him.[11] The letters indicate that his first attempts dealt rather directly with his problems with Frieda, that the manuscript grew alarmingly through additions and rewriting (he is repeatedly on the verge of "finishing" it), and that he finally had to divide "The Sisters" into two novels: *The Rainbow* and *Women in Love.* Characteristically everything was much rewritten, so that what we have now is probably not much like what was produced in 1913. But "the relation between men and women," we can be sure, was centrally present in all the drafts.

In both of the books which grew out of "The Sisters" Lawrence extends his range of experience. His interest in sexual relations is most fundamentally an interest in extending their meaning, not a mere fascination with their intensity. It is no surprise, then, that in *The Rainbow* sex is once again related to natural forces, nor is it a surprise that attempts are also made to relate it to the social and the cultural, especially the mining world out of which Lawrence came. What is perhaps surprising is the degree to which he succeeds in showing that sexual activity can provide a transcendence of one's usual self which allows direct apprehension of a fundamental unity in all life. How he does this can scarcely be summarized, since his success is very largely a matter of technique, but it is at least clear that beneath his success lies a growing confidence that such a unity is possible, however difficult it may be to describe or to discover. It is here that we encounter Lawrence calling himself a "religious" writer, and it is here that critics are inclined to agree with him.

The same need to extend human relations beyond the merely human shapes *Women in Love,* only the world in which it appears has changed radically. Here is the mood in which *The Rainbow* was completed.

> I had been walking in Westmorland, rather happy, with water-lilies twisted round my hat—big, heavy, white and gold water-lilies that we found in a pool high up—and girls who had come out on a spree and who were having tea in the upper room of an inn, shrieked with

[11] The serious work became *The Lost Girl,* published in 1920.

Introduction

laughter. And I remember also we crouched under the loose wall on the moors and the rain flew by in streams, and the wind came rushing through chinks in the wall behind one's head, and we shouted songs, and I imitated music-hall turns, whilst the other men crouched under the wall and I pranked in the rain on the turf in the gorse, and Koteliansky groaned Hebrew music—*Ranani Sadekim Badanoi.*

It seems like another life—we *were* happy—four men. Then we came down to Barrow-in-Furness, and saw that war was declared. And we all went mad.[12]

This captures, as well as anything Lawrence wrote, his belief, which many of his contemporaries later came to share, that the war dramatically transformed a world of gaiety into a world of madness. And precisely at the time when Lawrence's life and art both showed new promise of order and purpose, his countrymen declared his most ambitious novel filth.

I suggested earlier that Lawrence's dismay about the war is a measure of his optimism and expectation before it began. It is important also to note that, if optimism disappeared, hope did not. However much *Women in Love* may be a "destructive" book, two of its characters survive and even succeed, and these two characters represent Lawrence and Frieda. In their success we find articulated a conception of marriage which *The Rainbow* adumbrated in less coherent form.[13] It is clearly a conception toward which all of Lawrence's previous novels have also been tending, and it is entirely an affirmation of life. So if *Women in Love* contains, as Lawrence claimed, the results in his soul of the war, the war did not altogether "destroy" him. It did, however, encourage all Lawrence's tendencies toward isolation and escape. He sought to justify these tendencies in comprehensive criticisms of the civilization he fled, and he forcefully embodied them in *Women in Love.*

IV

There was, of course, a great deal to criticize in the recently mechanized civilization which produced catastrophe on a scale new in recorded history. And Lawrence, especially after the trial of *Lady Chatterley's Lover,* is now popularly known as a critic of mechanized society, inhabited largely by counterparts of Clifford Chatterley, intellectually active but paralyzed below the waist. But a careful reading of *Women in Love,* where Lawrence first articulated fully his indictment of a dying civilization, should make us formulate his criticisms

[12] *Letters,* I, 309.
[13] See especially the speech by Tom Brangwen at Anna's marriage.

a bit more carefully than either the friends or the enemies of *Lady Chatterley's Lover* could do in a British court room in 1960. Gerald Crich, who most fully embodies Lawrence's conviction that "destruction" had somehow become the prevalent mode of life, is a helpful example.

As Moynahan succinctly explains below, Gerald Crich seems doomed from the start. He seems almost a caricature, so fiercely inhibited by his mind and his will, so devoted to creating "organization" in the industrial world, that he drives himself to madness and suicide. Certainly Lawrence means us to understand that Gerald has pursued the materialistic values implicit in Victorian notions of "progress," found them meaningless, and discovered too late that some more fundamental meaning is necessary for life. Yet while all this is true, to recognize it does not reveal the extent of Lawrence's involvement with "destruction," nor does it help us explain why Gerald's death is a tragedy. How, after all, can we become involved with a man whose activity is so willed as to seem inhuman? The answer, of course, is that he is not "really" inhuman; he embodies possibility, as Lawrence's most destructive book embodies possibility. It is only with this possibility in mind that we can understand its destruction, just as it is necessary to look beneath Lawrence's responses to the war to understand why it was horrible to him.

We are given a more thorough account of Gerald's childhood and youth than of anyone else in the book. In a long chapter which some have found tedious, Lawrence takes trouble to explain Gerald's relation to his family and his mines. There are some good and obvious reasons for doing this: not only is Gerald the central representative in the book of the civilization Lawrence is rejecting, but he acts out in his person and his life not so much a mysterious lack of vitality (the "fated" circumstances which Moynahan describes so well) as a misplacement of it, an inadequacy which is a mistake as well as a fate. Although we must recognize from the start that vital inadequacies are ultimately mysterious, we can hardly feel Gerald's destruction strongly without noticing that he is a victim of circumstances which, in another book or another world, might have been different.

> In his travels, and in his accompanying readings, he had come to the conclusion that the essential secret of life was harmony. He did not define to himself at all clearly what harmony was. The word pleased him, he felt he had come to his own conclusions. And he proceeded to put his philosophy into practice by forcing order into the established world, translating the mystic word harmony into the practical word organisation. (p. 220) [14]

[14] References are to the Compass edition of *Women in Love* (New York: Viking, 1960).

Introduction 13

This is, perhaps, Gerald's most crucial mistake. His father, though less thoughtful, less philosophical, made one much like it by taking too simply the Christian idea of spiritual equality and forcing it to a "material" conclusion; he tried to translate it into egalitarianism. Gerald in turn "translates" the more abstract idea of "mystic harmony." In both instances the meaning of ideas which refer to spiritual values is misunderstood, with disastrous results. It is precisely in this way, Lawrence argues, that modern civilization persists in misunderstanding its goals. Materialism not only substitutes quantities for qualities; it reduces the sacred to the secular, unlimited possibility to possibilities of arrangement and manipulation. Gerald, at least, can claim some good intentions. He came to these conclusions by pursuing a legitimately vital urge to make sense of his world. Lawrence, moreover, makes clear that Gerald is more honest than his father. But his mistake is worse, for by it he confirms those tendencies toward destruction which are already implicit both in himself and in his miners.

These tendencies can be described as demonic. The word is invited by passages like this one:

> "It is like a country in an underworld," said Gudrun. "The colliers bring it above-ground with them, shovel it up. Ursula, it's marvellous, it's really marvellous—it's really wonderful, another world. The people are all ghouls, and everything is ghostly. Everything is a ghoulish replica of the real world, a replica, a ghoul, all soiled, everything sordid. It's like being mad, Ursula." (p. 5.)

This is Gudrun, responding with a thrill to a world with which she is shown in the course of the book to have many affinities, not the least of which is her attraction to Gerald.

> His gleaming beauty, maleness, like a young, good-humored smiling wolf, did not blind her to the significant, sinister stillness in his bearing, the lurking danger of his unsubdued temper. "His totem is the wolf," she repeated to herself. (p. 9.)

Gerald's sinister wolfishness is, among other things, a sign of his power. The underworld could not have been created without a real power in its creator, and this power is, like Gerald's inquisitiveness, a sign of life. But the whole enterprise amounts to something "ghoulish," not merely because it substitutes the material for the spiritual, but because it embodies real life seeking a perverted form. This, in fact, is what the demonic means in Lawrence's work: a misdirected vital energy, bent more on destruction than on creation.[15] All the characters in

---

[15] There are hints, both in *Women in Love* and in Lawrence's later works, that demonic energies may finally lead to some sort of purgation, to a death which gives new life. But this possibility is not fully articulated here. Kingsley Widmer has

Women in Love show some demonic tendency (the little animal Loerke is almost exclusively demonic), but only in Gerald is the perversion of real possibility thoroughly explored.

To confront this possibility more directly we need to inquire once again into Lawrence's purpose, his search for meaning. In *The Rainbow*, the quest for religious experience, an experience of self-transcendence and ultimately of unity, is predominantly focused on sexual relations. In *Women in Love*, a more determined effort is made to see all of life, including Gerald's mines, as part of a quest for the same ultimate relation. But here the results are predominantly negative. Although all the major characters of *Women in Love* possess some share of vitality (and in Lawrence vitality has always, taken alone, a positive value), only Ursula and Birkin find ways to direct it fruitfully. Hermione and Gudrun, in complementary ways, are determined to maintain defensive patterns of inhibition. Only Gerald significantly wavers, shows possibility that is tragically defeated. This is particularly evident when we contrast with Gudrun's his experience of sexual consummation (still the paradigm for the transcendent experience) after his father's death. He loses himself and finds a peace, a healing process seems to be taking place; she discovers an emptiness which keeps her awake. Unfortunately for Gerald, he depends upon Gudrun to foster what "true" vitality he has, and she does all she can to deny him further opportunities. She may even be said to murder him through her deliberate exploitation of his dependency. Although critics have emphasized strongly that Gerald invites this destruction and multiplies his mistakes,[16] it is no distortion to insist as well that his search for an "answer" is more determined and honest than Gudrun's and even shows chances of success.

These chances, however, despite good advice from Birkin, turn to failure for reasons that go beyond both Gerald's mistakes and his fated inheritance. The destructiveness of *Women in Love* consists not only in an indictment of a materialistic civilization, which prizes the intellect and the will above the less tangible values of vital freedom, responsiveness to nature and to others; it depicts that materialism as a manifestation of a larger, destructive movement. Just here, analysis of cause and effect becomes confused: did Lawrence proclaim doom because he responded violently to materialism and the war it produced, or did the war make him see something more fundamental?

---

enthusiastically pursued this aspect of Lawrence in his *The Act of Perversity* (Seattle: University of Washington Press, 1962), a study of Lawrence's short fiction.

[16] See Mark Schorer's "*Women in Love* and Death," in Mark Spilka, ed., *D. H. Lawrence: A Collection of Critical Essays* (Englewood Cliffs: Prentice-Hall, Inc., 1963), pp. 50–61.

Lawrence, of course, would have preferred the second formulation. Part of what he meant by his claim to be a religious writer was that he refused to be limited to explanations that depend upon analysis of efficient causes, be they historical or psychological. They tend to avoid the final problems of meaning and value, and these were problems Lawrence—even obsessively—found it necessary to confront. So it is not enough to say that Gerald Crich is doomed because he misdirects his vitality, or because others cause him to misdirect it. We must also say that he misdirects it because he has to function in a world that is itself dominated by demonic propensity, and his most important mistake is a failure to recognize this as clearly as Birkin does. When Gerald finds himself a "flower of dissolution," Birkin tells him what this means, but he refuses to accept Birkin's analysis. His refusal is an affirmation of secular limits, a deliberate withdrawal from a search for the meaning of experiences which cannot be "translated" into patterns he can manipulate. The whole relationship with Gudrun demonstrates such a refusal; he depends upon her precisely to the degree that he refuses to accept, to inquire into and understand, the difference between her vital capacity and his own, a difference clearly evident in scenes like that mentioned above. He refuses, in short, to conceive his life as a search for meaning that can have no set limits.[17] In this he differs from Lawrence's most vital protagonists, Tom Brangwen and Birkin. They "come through" not because they find final answers but because they remain aware that life is irreducibly mysterious, that its meaning must always be sought but will always remain finally "unknown."

V

There is of course some limitation to the continued questioning about "ultimates," especially since, Lawrentians or not, we refer by that word to a limit of understanding. Lawrence took such questioning with a seriousness unique among his generation, and it influences not only the presentation of Gerald but the more technical aspects of the novel as well, its modes of characterization and its larger patterns of organization. As anyone who has read even the first chapter can testify, there is something cryptic about our impressions of the characters. The sisters engage in curiously desultory talk about marriage and jumping off—where? Why does a man make marriage "impossible"? Or again, it is odd that a character should limp, as Birkin does, from self-consciousness. What is this "singleness" that he is guard-

[17] See Alan Friedman's essay below for some of the formal implications of this idea.

ing by behaving as if he were "quite ordinary"? These are questions that the novel sets out to answer at length, and they are not raised merely to arouse the reader's curiosity. The answers to these and many similar questions are to be sought by, once again, puzzling over "ultimates," which need not be as vague and obscure a process as it sounds. For the puzzling is done by the book itself, most dramatically in passages like this one.

> And then she experienced a keen paroxysm, a transport, as if she had made some incredible discovery, known to nobody else on earth. A strange transport took possession of her, all her veins were in a paroxysm of violent sensation. . . . She was tortured with desire to see him again, a nostalgia, a necessity to see him again, to make sure it was not all a mistake, that she was not deluding herself, that she really felt this strange and overwhelming sensation on his account, this knowledge of him in her essence, this powerful apprehension of him. (p. 9.)

This sort of language has offended some of Lawrence's readers. It can hardly be dispensed with, however, if Lawrence's purpose is to be understood and his effect appreciated. Terms like "transport," "paroxysm," and "knowledge . . . in her essence" refer, first, to what we would expect: a powerful sexual attraction. But beyond this they indicate that Gudrun's response involves her to the very grounds of her being, involves her essentially. Where this involvement leads, what it implies for Gudrun and others, is not understood by Gudrun here, nor is it "explained" until the whole book is read. But the very language indicates that explanation must not be limited either to the traditional psychology of love or to mere sensuality. Lawrence attempts with a new directness to reveal the quality of experience and to relate it to an essential core, which by this time in his career he had conceived as being *beneath* personality. What we see here in Gudrun is a direct, though momentary, exposure of this "core" (in one place Lawrence called it the "carbon" of character). The result of such experiences (which one may fruitfully compare to Joyce's epiphanies or Virginia Woolf's moments of vision) is always a profound shock and at least momentary loss of self. This is usually followed by reevaluation of the self, with the possibility of change newly imminent. In Lawrence change is usually of positive value; the characters who fail to change, like Gudrun, characteristically deny the revelations they receive in these transcendent experiences. Although we would distort Lawrence greatly by insisting that these experiences are themselves the "point" of his writing, we cannot understand him without recognizing that they are crucial to his characterization. Through them the characters are forced to confront a self without its usual defenses, the screen of ideas that obscures what one really is. For the reader of

Women in Love this means that a new, or at least unusual, kind of attention is needed. Beyond the usual psychological analysis ("Gerald depends too much on sex") he must attempt a "Lawrentian" ontological analysis ("Gerald has certain vital deficiencies which lead him to misuse sex"). Ideally, this latter analysis leads even to a new consciousness in the reader, which will allow him to understand directly the quality and meaning of these moments of revelation. This, at least, is what Lawrence hoped, and it is what his unsympathetic critics call impossible. Certainly it is difficult, but the book richly repays a little struggle.

Because Lawrence's search for meaning became increasingly comprehensive (at least through the novels we have noticed), it is also necessary to pay unusual attention to *inter*relationships in *Women in Love*. Of all of Lawrence's books, this is the most tightly and elaborately organized. As we read, the characters begin to group themselves according to their symbolic meanings, forming patterns which are again a result of Lawrence's concern to understand both destructiveness and possibility—in personal relationships, in civilization, even in life itself. Trying to capture some of the intricacy of Lawrence's thematic weaving, critics have called *Women in Love* a dialectic and also a dance.

Both words imply a movement of approach and opposition. The most comprehensive way to formulate this opposition is to notice that two patterns of imagery, each with extensive symbolic meaning, dominate characterization and description of the significant groups of people in the book. These images are as old as literature itself: light and darkness. But the meanings associated with them are not exactly the traditional ones. On the light side we have a group of characters (arranged here in descending order of intensity): Hermione, Gerald, Birkin. On the dark side another group: Loerke, Gudrun, Gerald, Ursula. The repetition of Gerald is not a mistake; it is intended to indicate that more than the others he belongs throughout the book to two worlds, almost evenly to each.

Light is associated with the mind, especially with its processes of abstraction and inhibition; darkness is associated with the senses, with violence, with the demonic as described above. So Hermione is more intellectual and inhibited than Gerald, who is more so than Birkin. And Loerke is more devoted to following sensual propensities than Gudrun, who is in turn more this way than Gerald or Ursula. On the other hand, there are complications in this scheme, and once again Gerald is helpful in examining them. Gerald, we have noticed, is extraordinarily "willed." His mind exerts more control than Birkin's, even though Birkin is, in the usual sense of the word, more of an intellectual. But he is not so willed as Hermione, as is evident from Birkin's attacks on her sexuality. Gudrun, too, is unusually willed, for she keeps her sensuality under great control. "Will" often means in Lawrence precisely this rigidity and control. It is not always a pejorative term, though in *Women in Love* it usually is, since the problem with which all the characters grapple is conceived as a problem of release into freedom from rigid forms. So Gerald, who is caught in a rigid (and ultimately empty) sensuality, is also caught in a rigid sort of intellectualism in the "translation" we noticed him make. He is described as "arctic" and "gleaming," and he also has "dark power." Gudrun is much more consistently involved in narcissistic, sensual activity; she has no corresponding intellectualism. And Loerke, though in his theories of art (which he shares with Gudrun) very intellectual indeed, is described as a whole menagerie of animals, most strikingly as a sewer rat.

There are two major modes, then, of willed behavior in the novel: that of the intellectual, who abstracts and thereby both falsifies and inhibits natural impulse (Hermione in the classroom is a good example of this), and that of the sensualist, who channels his energies by deliberate exclusion of humanistic concern, and therefore becomes both narcissistic and destructive. Since *Women in Love* places its central values in the search for "fulfillment," both extremes—violence and sensuality on one hand, abstraction and intellectuality on the other— become identical in misdirecting natural vitality. This identity is repeatedly demonstrated in the book, not merely in the figure of Gerald. Hermione, the most willed and abstracted of all, achieves a demonic and homicidal release when she attacks Birkin; Loerke, the least "human" of them all, rationalizes his sensuality as "pure" art. And the whole last section of the book, those chapters which take place on the continent, insists through its frozen setting for violence that both extreme modes come, ultimately, to the same thing. Gudrun is perhaps our best example here. The snow-tipped peaks induce a "final" ecstasy in her, a perverted mode of the transcendent experience which Birkin seeks. She finds that she desires this self-annihilation more than she desires Gerald, who would still awaken her to self-responsibility. Loerke, who makes no such demands, offers himself as substitute. So Gerald is destroyed, and we are made conscious both through the mode of his "murder" and the repulsiveness of the new coupling that abstraction (here taken to the "logical" extreme of self-annihilation) and sensuality (here embodied in a significantly "intellectualized" form, an art which exploits sexuality while denying its relation to life) are both destructive, both rooted in the same fear of discovering one's true "being."

The only persistent attempt at this sort of discovery is, of course, that of Ursula and Birkin, who move in the course of the book away from these extremes toward some sort of balance, which Birkin finally formulates in his ideas of equilibrium in marriage. He argues there for a form of transcendence that is neither narcissistic (like Gudrun's) nor dependent (like Gerald's). The success of this doctrine depends upon the ability of the marriage partners to achieve a transcendence which, while freeing them from the pettiness of their everyday selves, allows them to remain separate, not "merged" (the mode of more traditional romantic love). It may be disputed whether, or how fully, they succeed in convincing us of the viability of this doctrine.[18] But whatever reservations we may hold, it is clear that Ursula and Birkin carry the positive thrust of the book. They also provide a refutation of those who equate Lawrence's values entirely with a mindless vitalism, for the main mode through which they come together is talk and argument—intellectual modes, a kind of dialectic in itself. They must, of course, finally give up their talk and come together directly, sexually. But their meeting presupposes a mutual understanding which had to be talked out.

This brings us back to the use of "dialectic" to refer to the structure of *Women in Love*. There are at least two basic ways in which the term may be applied: it can refer simply to the argument which goes on between Ursula and Birkin, an argument which develops through both intellectual and emotional oppositions, sometimes violent, but finally achieving a kind of resolution. It can also refer to the thematic opposition between intellectuality and sensuality which we have been noticing. The latter opposition resolves itself in destruction, apparently signifying a dismissal of the whole secular civilization against which Lawrence is here rebelling. This dismissal is not, however, final: the question at the end remains a genuine question, referring not merely to Gerald but also to the need for more definition, more of a clear positive direction, for Lawrence's protagonists as well as for Lawrence himself. Lawrence's next novels prove that the fate of civilization could not be dismissed from his mind, however much he might continue to complain and flee. Yet of all his novels, this one remains the most impressive indictment of the mechanistic world from which he fled, an indictment which arose directly out of his extraordinary need to establish an inclusive and human one.

[18] David Gordon has reservations; see pp. 50–60.

PART ONE

Interpretations

Dies Irae

by George H. Ford

That *The Rainbow* has dimensions beyond the level of naturalistic narrative was indicated (in a previous discussion) by showing how extensively Lawrence established analogies between the experiences of the Brangwens and various incidents in the Bible. In this respect *Women in Love* has an even more elaborate frame of reference, for instead of the comparisons being restricted to the story of one people—the race of Israel—the comparisons this time are expanded to take in many peoples and nations. The analogy between London and Sodom is recurrently made in *Women in Love,* yet the Bible story of how a certain corrupt civilization was destroyed is, in this novel, only one of many stories and histories being drawn upon. How civilizations die, or might die, is the subject of *Women in Love*—not how the course of one civilization is like that of one other civilization—which was treated in *The Rainbow.* The differences between the two novels derive not only from the author's awareness of the war, but from his more extended use of history, prehistory, and myth in the later work. The history of Israel still provides parallels but expanded now by an awareness of other past civilizations: Rome, Carthage, Greece, Egypt, Babylon, the legendary Atlantis, and the lost city states of Africa.

One can readily understand why Virginia Woolf could have gained the impression that Lawrence "never looked back at the past" and also why a later critic, J. H. Raleigh, asserts that "Joyce stands for history, Lawrence for futurity," [1] yet both estimates are misleading. Man's past, or perhaps more precisely *his* impression of man's past, was crucially important to Lawrence. Murray's book on Greek religions

---

From "Dies Irae" by George H. Ford. From Double Measure: A Study of the Novels and Stories of D. H. Lawrence *(New York: Holt, Rinehart and Winston, Inc., 1965), pp. 184–207. Copyright © 1965 by George H. Ford. Reprinted with minor revisions by the author by permission of Holt, Rinehart and Winston, Inc.*

[1] Virginia Woolf, *The Moment and other Essays,* p. 82, and J. H. Raleigh in *Partisan Review* (1958), p. 260.

annoyed him as did H. G. Wells' history by their assumptions about the inferiority of the past. As Achsah Brewster noted: "The old gods were as important to Lawrence as the new, different but not inferior." [2] Or as the leading character in his story "Glad Ghosts" says: "my desire to go onwards takes me back a little."

It must be recalled that like Dickens, with his pot-boiler production, *A Child's History of England,* Lawrence ventured into writing a volume of history, setting to work on it shortly after he had completed *Women in Love.* Published in 1921, his *Movements of European History* confirms what is evident elsewhere in his writing, that minute historical accuracies were of little concern to him. The "broken-pots of historical facts" bored him, he said, but in writing his history he deeply enjoyed trying to locate "the thread of the developing significance" of past events.[3] The past he treated in the same way as he treated countries such as Sardinia or New Mexico in his travel books; by its store of examples of cultures similar to our own, or different from our own, the past provided him with an opportunity for impressionistic speculations on the nature of man, and on man's probable fate. His keen interest in anthropological studies was similarly inspired. Hence in his reading he tended to prefer accounts of epochs or peoples about which our store of information is not altogether precise. Of the Etruscans he noted: "That which half emerges from the dim background of time is strangely stirring." [4]

This interest in the history and legends of past civilizations was keenly intensified during the years of the war. Shortly before its outbreak in 1914 he had planned to spend a month reading in the library at the British Museum in order to prepare for his "next novel." These proposed researches had to be postponed until moving to Cornwall in 1916, where in relative isolation, he settled down to an intensive course of reading which he was to pursue for many months until, and after, he began writing this "next novel" in late April, 1916. As a result *Women in Love* is, in the jargon of the social sciences, one of the more *researched* of English novels.

In view of his mood of wartime despair, one might expect Lawrence, at this time, to have sought anodynes in his reading. The reverse was true. In requesting friends to send books, he specified that he did not want to read novels or poetry or "belles lettres." [5] Instead of fiction he

---

[2] Nehls, III, 403.
[3] *Letters* (Huxley), p. 466. See also Philip Rieff's essay "A Modern Mythmaker" in *Myth and Mythmaking,* ed. Henry A. Murray (New York, 1960), pp. 240–75.
[4] *Etruscan Places* (1932), p. 44.
[5] *Letters,* I, 416. The only fiction he seems to have read during this period was Melville's *Moby Dick,* about which he was enthusiastic, and some novels of Dostoevsky, which he professed to find distasteful (perhaps in part to deflate John Middleton Murry's reverential attitude to the Russian master).

was soaking himself in works of history, anthropology, mythology, and ethnology. On January 21, 1916, he asked Koteliansky to bring him books on "Norse or Anglo Saxon or early Celtic" cultures, studies of "Orphic religions, or Egypt, or on anything really African." And by April 1, he reported to Kot that his head was now full of "Greek translations and Ethnology" rather than "stories."

More specifically, he read Frazer's *Golden Bough* and *Totemism and Exogamy*, and Sir Edward Tylor's *Primitive Culture* (these following an earlier reading of Jane Harrison's *Ancient Art and Ritual*—"you have no idea how much I got out of that . . . book," he reported). A *History of the East* with its account of the "crashing down of nations and empires" impressed him and led to his reading a history of early Egypt and also Niccolao Manucci's *History of the Mogul Dynasty in India* which made him realize that "these Hindus are horribly decadent and reverting to all forms of barbarism in all sorts of ugly ways." [6] He was also led (when he could bear it, he said) to Thucydides where he had to confront "the fact of these wars of a collapsing era." "It is too horrible to see a people . . . fling itself down the abyss of the past, and disappear." [7] His response to Thucydides (whom Birkin in the novel is represented as reading when Hermione tries to murder him) indicates the spirit in which Lawrence undertook his program of study. "The Peloponnesian war was the death agony of Greece." "*All* Greece died. It must not be so again." A knowledge of past civilizations and of cultures in other continents provided a Spenglerian perspective on the crumbling world of 1916, and in particular on what seemed to Birkin, in the novel, "the dying body" of English civilization itself:

> "You think the English will have to disappear?" persisted Gudrun. It was strange, her pointed interest in his answer. It might have been her own fate she was inquiring after. [386]

To know how Gudrun might die, how England and the western world might die, history and legend were helpfully informative, although not comforting.

How was this store of reading put to use in *Women in Love*? When Ibsen was asked what he had been reading he is reported to have replied that he read nothing; he was a writer. Lawrence would

---

[6] *Letters*, I, 451–52. Cf. the account of Halliday's "aristocratic-looking" Hindu servant in *Women in Love*: "Birkin felt a slight sickness, looking at him, and feeling the slight greyness as an ash or a corruption."—It is also worth noting that even with his relatively small cast of characters Lawrence was able to introduce enough foreigners, Russian, German, Hindu, to suggest that the fate of man, rather than just the fate of England, is at stake.

[7] *Letters*, I, 249, 416, 424, 425, 436, 451, 454, 466, 468.

not have subscribed to such nonsense, but he was also aware that an author's reading can swamp his book if it is dumped there in its raw state. George Eliot's *Romola* is a painful example of what happens when laborious researches remain unincorporated into fiction, and Lawrence's own *Plumed Serpent* suffers, at times, from the same failing. In *Women in Love,* on the contrary, the information and insights gleaned by the author from Tylor and Thucydides become integrated components of a picture. Rarely discussed directly (like the war which is never mentioned) they add immeasurably to the scope of his story of a sick society.

II

In Chapter XI Ursula Brangwen listens to Birkin's thunderings on the degeneration of hate-filled modern man. At times she is impressed; at other times, like her mother in the solemnity of the cathedral in *The Rainbow,* she is amused. A crucial point in their argument occurs, however, when he is predicting a day of wrath in which humanity will be quickly wiped out. She disagrees. "She knew it could not disappear so cleanly and conveniently. It had a long way to go yet, a long and hideous way. Her subtle, feminine, demoniacal soul knew it well." If the many references to cataclysm in *Women in Love* suggest the impact of war, this reference to an alternative doom for mankind, the "long way," the slow decline into extinction, suggests in general the influence of the novelist's reading. But what is Ursula supposed to mean by her mysterious and fearsome reference to this "long and hideous way?" Does the novel ever explain what is meant or are we left, as Conrad leaves us in his *Heart of Darkness,* shuddering at the implications of Kurtz's famous phrase—"The horror! the horror!"— without our ever clearly knowing what the horror is?

I think we can come close to identifying what the horror is in Lawrence's book although his commentators seem rarely to have been concerned with the problem. It could, of course, be maintained that the inquiry should not be pushed, because readers may be more powerfully affected by something sensed, imprecisely, as elusively threatening, than by an identifiable threat. The poems of Coleridge, a master of the rhetoric of horror, could be cited to reinforce the objection:

> Behold! her bosom and half her side—
> A sight to dream of, not to tell!
> O shield her! shield sweet Christabel!

Nevertheless, because many of the misunderstandings of *Women in Love* originate in an inadequate recognition of what the horror, or horrors, might be, we must risk this not very significant loss and seek out a confrontation.

These remarks must serve as a preamble to a consideration of a scene in chapter XIX of major importance as embodying the climax of one of the two main plot lines. In one respect the scene resembles the "Nightmare" chapter in *Kangaroo* inasmuch as every study of Lawrence refers to it without any agreement having been arrived at. The problem here, however, is not one of liking or disliking (it is generally admired); the problem is one of interpretation and understanding. The scene embodies a kind of soliloquy in the third person, with Birkin confronting, in his mind's eye, an African carving he had contemplated many times at Halliday's flat in London. Like the scene of the doctor's descent into the pond-water in "The Horse Dealer's Daughter," it is climactic in that after the confrontation or descent the character reaches a major decision. Birkin's experience culminates immediately in his resolving to marry Ursula, and as he sets out for her house to make his proposal, the ugly town of Beldover seems to him radiantly beautiful. "It looked like Jerusalem to his fancy," as Christminster ("the heavenly Jerusalem") looked to Hardy's Jude. Before the resolution is reached and the brief epiphany experienced, Birkin has to make a deep descent.

Among the African fetish statues he had seen in Halliday's London apartment, Birkin remembers one of a woman, a "slim, elegant figure from West Africa, in dark wood, glossy and suave. . . . He remembered her vividly: she was one of his soul's intimates." Why is it that the statue had haunted Birkin so persistently? Like many of his generation in the western world, Birkin enjoys African carving for its aesthetic satisfactions, yet it is obvious that his almost obsessive concern is not motivated by a search for beauty. It is what these statues tell him about the history of civilization and of his own future:

> He remembered her; her astonishing cultured elegance, her diminished, *beetle face,* the astounding long elegant body, on short, ugly legs, with such *protuberant buttocks,* so weighty and unexpected below her slim long loins. She knew *what he himself did not know.* She had thousands of years of purely sensual, purely unspiritual knowledge behind her. It must have been thousands of years since her race had died, mystically: that is, since the relation between the senses and the outspoken mind had broken, leaving the experience all in one sort, mystically sensual. Thousands of years ago, *that which was imminent in himself* must have taken place in these Africans: the goodness, the holiness, the desire for creation and productive happiness must have lapsed, leaving the single impulse for knowledge in one sort . . . in disintegration and dissolution, knowledge such as the beetles have. [Italics mine.]

Birkin's reflections serve as a flashback to the earlier scene in Halliday's apartment when another African statue was seen, this time through the eyes of Gerald. He, too, is disturbed by the statue (it is of a woman in labor), and although he finds no aesthetic pleasure he nevertheless senses what Birkin associated with it. It conveys to Gerald "the suggestion of the extreme physical sensation, beyond the limits of mental consciousness." [8] The early scene of the breakfast party is memorably staged with the four naked men standing round the statue and commenting on the "terrible face, void, peaked, abstracted almost into meaninglessness by the weight of sensation beneath." And the affair of the preceding night is also effectively incorporated by Gerald's significant discovery that the statue makes him think of the Pussum, the "violated slave" still asleep in the adjacent bedroom. But Gerald makes one blunder in his response to the statue. He thinks it is crude and savage. Birkin hastens to correct him:

"There are centuries and hundreds of centuries of development in a straight line, behind that carving; it is an awful pitch of culture, of a definite sort." [72]

Gerald's mistake is one often made by those readers of Lawrence who overlook what Birkin calls the "astonishing cultured elegance" of the statue and assume that he is evoking a work by a savage. Such a reading blurs the main point of his soliloquy. Lawrence had learned from his reading (and his subsequent study of Leo Frobenius' *The Voice of Africa* confirmed the point) that long before the coming of Europeans there had existed great city states in Africa which had produced highly sophisticated works of art and established a tradition

[8] In this discussion I am quoting from the original version of *Women in Love* (London, 1921) before Pussum was changed into Minette. The revisions which Lawrence introduced into his later edition were prompted by the threat of a libel suit, and although a few of them might reflect a more significant change of intention, most of them are mere insulators, and not being consistently changed, they also lead to confusion. Because Heseltine, who was threatening the libel suit, had African statues in his apartment, Lawrence obliged by changing the one referred to in chapters VI and VII into a statue from the West Pacific and by deleting the references to Negroes. But in chapter XIX he left these unchanged. See also his reference in an essay to "an African fetish idol of a woman pregnant" (*Reflections on the Death of a Porcupine*, pp. 140–41). At least from our present perspective, one detail of these revisions is an amusing example of Lawrence's humor. The name *Pussum* was changed to *Minette* presumably because Heseltine's mistress had been known as the Puma, but the name of Heseltine's wife, whom he married in December, 1916, was *Minnie* Channing. And to compound his sly jest in changing the name and yet retaining its original connotations, Lawrence makes capital of the fact that the word *minette,* in French, is the equivalent of the word *pussy* in English.

of fine craftsmanship.⁹ A slow decline, not a cataclysm, finished off this civilization, and it is the nature of this decline that Birkin tries to conjure up as he contemplates what the statue symbolizes for him.

Parenthetically it should be added that, so far as our appreciation of *Women in Love* is concerned, it does not matter fundamentally whether Birkin is right or wrong in his information about disputed points of Africa's past. Nor does it matter fundamentally whether his assumptions about one of the ways a civilization may decline are accurate or inaccurate. They are part of the given world of this novel and essential to an understanding of it. The basic assumption, and one developed in the parody scene at the Pompadour when Birkin's letter is read aloud by Halliday, is that a civilization having evolved out of its savage beginnings may lose its creative urge and lapse into decadence before becoming simply extinct. "There is a phase in every race— . . . when the desire for destruction overcomes every other desire." As intoned by the drunken Halliday for the amusement of London's Bohemia (this "menagerie of apish degraded souls"), the effect of the pronouncement is painfully comic—painful because no other direct statement in *Women in Love* is more significant or more serious—and astringently comic because of the setting in which it is framed. If the social process so conceived is unchecked a civilization declines to a stage which may have some resemblance to the original savage stage; it suffers a "reduction"—an abstract term upon which Lawrence leans often and hard in his fiction and letters.

Writing to his Jewish friend Mark Gertler, whose "obscene" painting seems to have inspired the account of Loerke's frieze of the drunken workers in the novel, Lawrence uses the same historical formula: "You are of an older race than I, and in these ultimate processes, you are beyond me. . . . At last your race is at an end—these pictures are its death-cry. And it will be left for the Jews to utter the final . . . death-cry of this epoch: the Christians are not *reduced* sufficiently." ¹⁰ And in "St. Mawr" he restates more explicitly the assumptions on which these gloomy predictions are based:

> Every new stroke of civilization has cost the lives of countless brave men, who have fallen . . . in their efforts to overcome the old, half-sordid savagery of the lower stages of creation, and win to the next stage. . . . And every civilization, when it loses its inward vision and its cleaner energy, falls into a new sort of sordidness, more vast and more stupendous than the old savage sort.

---

⁹ On April 18, 1918, Lawrence wrote that he had read "two ponderous tomes on Africa" by Frobenius, and in *Aaron's Rod* he pictures Lilly reading the same author. —See also Basil Davidson, *The Lost Cities of Africa* (Boston, 1959), and André Malraux, *The Voices of Silence* (New York, 1953), p. 132.

¹⁰ *Letters*, I, 477–78. (Italics mine.)

During the composition of *Women in Love* Lawrence discovered some living illustrations much closer at hand than the Africans for his theory of cultural degeneration. His Cornish neighbors impressed him as a surviving pocket of a once impressive "pre-Christian Celtic civilisation" which had degenerated. In view of the beetle-like face of the African statue, the following description of the Cornish people (whose souls, he said, were like black beetles) is especially interesting:

> The aristocratic principle and the principle of magic, to which they belonged, these two have collapsed, and left only the most ugly, scaly, insect-like, unclean *selfishness*. . . . Nevertheless . . . there is left some of the old sensuousness of the darkness . . . something almost negroid, which is fascinating. But curse them, they are entirely mindless.[11]

This cluster associating the Celtic and African reappears in *Lady Chatterley's Lover* in a description of another Celt, the Irishman Michaelis:

> She saw in him that ancient motionlessness of a race that can't be disillusioned any more, an extreme, perhaps, of impurity that is pure, . . . he seemed pure, pure as an African ivory mask that dreams impurity into purity, in its ivory curves and planes.

That the African statues signify for Birkin a whole process of decline and fall, and that however aesthetically pleasing they evoke for him the impurity of a degenerated civilization, are points I have been laboring partly because of an extraordinary discussion of these statues by Horace Gregory in his *Pilgrim of the Apocalypse*. According to Gregory, Lawrence found his principal characters of less interest than the statue of the West African woman, "for him, perhaps the most important figure in the book."

> She is positive, concrete, the perfect representation of life as opposed to the imperfect human beings surrounding her. . . . What the statue is made to represent is the *normal* essence of Gudrun and Ursula combined —their deviation from the statue's norm . . . is the perversion imposed upon them by their individual existence. . . . In all four characters, male and female, the statue sets the standard, never fully realized by any of them.[12]

And Mr. Gregory concludes his analysis by asserting that "the image of the West African savage" was a fragment of hope in the midst of death. When a perceptive critic blunders into stating something so fantastically wrong as this (and other critics share his view) one is led to labor a point. Birkin's reflections in his soliloquy, developing like

---

[11] *Letters*, I, 418, and *Letters* (Huxley), pp. 303, 329.
[12] Horace Gregory, *D. H. Lawrence: Pilgrim of the Apocalypse* (New York, 1933), pp. 45-46, 49.

Keats, in his address to the Grecian urn, continues, and we may well ask what fragment of hope is there here:

> There is a long way we can travel, after the death-break; . . . We fall from the connection with life and hope, we lapse . . . into the long, long African process of purely sensual understanding . . . He realised now that this is a long process—thousands of years it takes, after the death of the creative spirit. He realised that there were great mysteries to be unsealed, sensual, mindless, dreadful mysteries, far beyond the phallic cult. How far, in their inverted culture, had these West Africans gone beyond phallic knowledge? Very, very far. Birkin recalled again the female figure: the elongated, long, long body, the curious unexpected heavy buttocks . . . the face with tiny features like a beetle's. This was far beyond any phallic knowledge. [246]

Only when Birkin makes his resolution to repudiate the direction pointed by the statue does the rhythm of hope make itself felt.

This much is clear, but the passage of Birkin's reflections remains one of the most puzzling in the novel. What is meant by the repeated references to some kind of knowledge "beyond phallic knowledge"? What is it that the woman knew that Birkin does not yet know but dreads he will know? The horror for Birkin is not the state of mindlessness itself. The term *mindlessness* appears often in Lawrence's writings to describe the state of darkness in which the Brangwen farmers live or the coal miners in *Sons and Lovers*. That a degenerating culture loses contact with the values of light and abandons the quest for intellectual effort (the quest portrayed in *The Rainbow*) may be deplorable but not terrifying and threatening, as in Birkin's reflections about the "dreadful mysteries far beyond the phallic cult." The latter seems to be the horror, the horror, in *Women in Love*. Whatever it is, three things may be said of it which call for more extended discussion. It involves some form (or rather forms) of sexual perversion; Birkin is strongly attracted to it (as the Pussum said of Birkin's sermon, "Oh, he was always talking about Corruption. He must be corrupt himself, to have it so much on his mind."). And thirdly, its culmination is death itself, or more specifically some form of suicide, individual and national.

The first point, about sexual perversions, is the most difficult to establish, and even raising the question is enough to rouse the ire of some brands of Laurentian admirers. The difficulty is that the novel itself is not explicit, could not be explicit, in this area, and we have to grope our way up a rickety ladder constructed of image-clusters and scraps of information. Halliday's mistress, the Pussum for example, is explicitly associated with the corruption when Lawrence says of her: "She was very handsome, flushed, and confident in dreadful knowledge." Less explicitly, a link is established by references to marsh flowers (she is "soft, unfolded like some red lotus in dreadful flowering nakedness,") and she is associated with the beetle-faced statue not so much by her fear of beetles but by her very appearance as in this remarkable passage:

> There was something curiously indecent, obscene, about her small, longish, dark skull, particularly when the ears showed.

Like many of the characters in *Women in Love* the Pussum is a vividly realized fictional creation yet at the same time, as representative of the corruption which the book treats, she is tagged by the novelist with evaluative terms such as *obscene*.

Gudrun Brangwen, a more highly complex character, is similarly presented. Her wood carvings were thought by Gerald to have been made by the same hands as those which created the African statues, and indeed Gudrun's affinities with what the statues suggested to Birkin are referred to many times. Most explicitly there is a passage near the end of the novel which is a kind of commentary on the earlier soliloquy. The passage consists of reflections (virtually a soliloquy again) on the difference between what Gerald offers as a lover of Gudrun and the kind of experience that Loerke could give her. Gerald's love-making has many qualities of perversity, but because he still has some "attachment" to moral virtues, "goodness" and "righteousness," he cannot provide the special sexual thrills that Loerke promises:

> Was it sheer blind force of passion that would satisfy her now? Not this, but the subtle thrills of extreme sensation in reduction. It was . . . the last subtle activities of . . . breaking down, carried out in the darkness of her. [442–43]

She reflects further that she no longer wants a man such as Gerald but a *"creature"* like Loerke (who had been described by Birkin as a sewer rat and by Gerald as an insect):

> The world was finished now, for her. There was only the inner, individual darkness . . . the *obscene religious mystery* of ultimate reduction, the mystic frictional activities of diabolic reducing down, disintegrating the vital organic body of life. . . . She had . . . a further, slow exquisite experience to reap, unthinkable subtleties of sensation to know, before she was finished. [Italics mine.]

Before an attempt is made to explicate Gudrun's soliloquy a word should be interjected about Loerke himself. Better even than the Pussum and Gudrun, Loerke illustrates Lawrence's bold technique of creating characters who are fully alive and so eloquently self-assertive that they may engage our sympathies, and yet, in terms of the book's overall theme, of exposing them as appalling examples of social corruption. It is almost a tightrope-walking performance, and one can see why some of these creations have aroused divergent responses in his readers. Loerke was even described by Nathan Scott (who sees Lawrence through the spectacles of Denis de Rougemont) as a "Laurentian saint." And to Anaïs Nin also, simply because he is an artist, he is the man to be admired. Of the fact that at the end of the book Gerald is dead and Loerke alive, Miss Nin says:

> So it is Gerald who dies, not Loerke. It is the "mindless sensuality" which dies. Yet it has been said that Lawrence in *Women in Love* had urged us to mindless sensuality and disintegration.[13]

The title of Miss Nin's book is *D. H. Lawrence: An Unprofessional Study,* and one wonders just how far the saving clause of her subtitle can be extended. Perhaps the most important equipment for a reader of Lawrence is just a nose. After his affair with the Pussum, Gerald admitted to Birkin:

> There's a certain smell about the skin of those women, that in the end is sickening beyond words—even if you like it at first.[14]

Lawrence surely expects us to be similarly responsive, and a reader who concludes that Loerke is a Laurentian saint would seem to be lacking in a sense of smell. "He lives like a rat, in the river of corruption, just where it falls over into the bottomless pit," says Birkin. Mankind, he adds, wants "to explore the sewers," and Loerke is "the wizard rat that swims ahead." His very name evokes his negativism, the Loki of the sagas and of William Morris's *Sigurd the Volsung:* "And Loki, the World's Begrudger, who maketh all labour vain."

What is it then that this ruthless little "creature" can provide that Gerald cannot offer? Both men have sadistic propensities and can presumably furnish the masochistic satisfactions that Gudrun craves. When she sees a picture of Loerke's nude statue of the young girl art-student on horseback (his preferences in girl-flesh anticipate those of the hero of Nabokov's *Lolita*), a girl who had to be subdued by his slapping her hard, "Gudrun went pale, and a darkness came over her eyes, like shame, she looked up with a certain supplication, *almost slave-like.*" The counterpointing here is extremely intricate, for we are reminded that perhaps the two high points of Gudrun's earlier appreciation of Gerald had been when she watched him subdue a rabbit by force or, more pertinently, when he drove his spurs into the

---

[13] Anaïs Nin, *D. H. Lawrence* (Paris, 1932), p. 110. See also Nathan A. Scott, Jr., *Rehearsals of Discomposure* (1952), p. 157.

[14] Cf. a reference to the women of the South Sea Island whose skin he could not conceive of touching: "flesh like warm mud. Nearer the reptile, the Saurian age." —*Studies in Classic American Literature* (New York, 1923), pp. 202–203.

flanks of his mare (scenes which will be discussed more extensively in my final chapter). And the phrase *almost slave-like* also flashes back to the Pussum whose submissive response to Gerald was similarly described.

Both men, then, have this capacity in common. What Loerke is capable of beyond it is the provision of some perverse pleasures, and the cluster of associations is consistently hinting at some exploitation of the anal and excremental areas. The recurring references to the abnormally prominent buttocks of the African statue and to sexual relations in which the connections with "creative life" are severed (anal intercourse has long been practised as a mode of avoiding conception), the traditional association of beetles with excrement, and the allusions to Loerke as a creature of the sewers all contribute towards some explication of both Birkin's soliloquy and that of Gudrun.

The hints concerning anal relations between men and women do not, however, indicate the full extent of the "further sensual experience" which Birkin contemplated. Gudrun's soliloquy, in particular, refers to some "obscene *religious* mystery of ultimate reduction." What is the term *religious* meant to suggest to us? Are we supposed to conjure up some Black Mass? Loerke, one might add, is well named to make a celebrant in such a rite, for in some Norse myths *Loki* is the devil. Perhaps it is merely the Bacchic festivals that are hinted at, or bestial erotic ceremonials,[15] or blood-sacrifice ceremonies such as the Druids had performed, or so Lawrence believed, in Cornwall. Somers in *Kangaroo* recalls his experience during 1916 in Cornwall of drifting into a "blood-darkness." "Human sacrifice!—he could feel his dark, blood-consciousness tingle to it again, the desire of it, the mystery of it." Again Conrad's *Heart of Darkness* provided a model (if a somewhat obscure one) in its allusions to Kurtz's participation in "certain midnight dances ending with unspeakable rites, which . . . were offered up to him." All that can be indicated about the introduction of the term *religious* into Lawrence's account of cultural degradation is that it reinforces a sense of the sinister without clarifying the nature of the corruption.

A further set of associations is less obscure but for Lawrence equally sinister, one that suggests that a declining society will revert to homosexuality. Loerke's perversities might include his love-hate relationship with his "companion" Leitner—they had for long shared a bedroom and "now reached the stage of loathing"—but this remains unde-

---

[15] So far as I know there is no record of Lawrence's being exposed to some library of erotic literature such as Swinburne was exposed to under the guidance of R. M. Milnes. His distaste for such writers as Casanova ("he smells") is well known. *Letters* (Huxley), p. 523.

veloped. The problem of homosexuality takes us back from Gudrun and Loerke to Birkin's soliloquy and its expression of anxieties.

Unlike Proust, whose novels of this period also treat of the Cities of the Plain, Lawrence elected to avoid any direct representation in *Women in Love* of what Ezekiel calls the "abomination" of Sodom; he offers us no study of a M. de Charlus. The Bohemians are described as "degenerate," and there is some emphasis on the men being effeminate in manner with high-pitched squealing voices, but if London is to be likened to Sodom it is more because of its probable future fate than its present condition in this respect. If for the moment we shift from the novel to the novelist, however, we may detect a figure in this carpet. Lawrence's letters of 1915 and 1916 contain a remarkable number of references to his horror of beetles which is related, in most instances, to a horror of homosexual relations. In the Moore edition of the letters alone there are eighteen references to beetles and insects during the years 1915–16. On April 30, 1915, he reported his disgust after seeing an "obscene" crowd of soldiers:

> I like men to be beasts—but insects—one insect mounted on another—oh God! The soldiers at Worthing are like that—they remind me of lice or bugs.

Most revealing are passages referring to a visit paid by Francis Birrell to the Lawrences (in the company of David Garnett):

> These horrible little frowsty people, men lovers of men, they give me such a sense of corruption, almost putrescence, that I dream of beetles.[16]

On this particular occasion his revulsion took form in an incident that as reported by Garnett, seems fantastic. So wrought up was Lawrence by Birrell's visit that he struggled to cast a spell over him, and the young man actually woke up at night with his tongue swollen so abnormally that he was in great pain.[17] As Lawrence himself reported, such young men "are cased each in a hard little shell of his own," and "they made me dream of a beetle that bites like a scorpion. But I killed it." One may associate the incident with Kafka, but much more striking is a similarity to the situation in *Genesis* when the men of Sodom gather outside Lot's house and demand that his guests, two angels, be delivered to the crowd "that we may know them." The guests retaliate on the men of Sodom by striking them with blindness—this on the night before the destruction of their city.

Francis Birrell was not the only man to provoke the beetle nightmare in Lawrence at this time. For some reason his unhappy visit to Cambridge led to his associating Keynes and the whole group there

[16] *Letters*, I, 333.
[17] Nehls, I, 269, 301.

with beetles and corruption, and also with Cambridge were linked such Bloomsbury figures as Duncan Grant.[18] In a letter to Henry Savage in December, 1913, in which he frankly aired his feelings about homosexual relations, Lawrence concluded:

> One is kept by all tradition and instinct from loving men, or a man—for it means just *extinction of all the purposive influences.*

It may be noted that the phrase which I have italicized is almost identical with the words used by Birkin in confronting the beetle-faced statue. As he contemplates the possible lapse from "the desire for creation and productive happiness," he speaks of the fall "from the connection with life and hope."

In this reconstruction of what is implied in Birkin's fearsome sense of the slow degeneration of western man, nothing so far has been said about machinery. So much has been written by others about Lawrence's vitalistic dislike of industrialism (and I shall add my mite in discussing Gerald Crich) that it is perhaps a useful corrective to see that the horror in *Women in Love* is not exclusively industrialism, against which Lawrence's nineteenth-century predecessors in this role, Carlyle, Ruskin, Morris, had already expended themselves in valiant invectives. It is manifested rather in various forms of sexual corruption. The degeneration of the African civilization, or of Sodom, did not depend upon the discovery of power-operated lathes or steam shovels. Industrialism may accelerate and will certainly complicate the process, but from his study of history and legend, Lawrence was aware of patterns of human propensities that were independent of how coal and iron are worked, and the differences between what he calls the African process and the Arctic process are not crucial. The end of the slow process of degeneration of past societies was extinction, and a degenerate contemporary society would descend the same slope.

The image of the death-slope is Lawrence's of course rather than mine. It crops up in the novel and also in several of his wartime letters. In August, 1915, he commented brutally on the kind of young man who joins the Roman Catholic Church, or the army, in order to enjoy obeying orders as a "swine with cringing hindquarters." [19] "I

---

[18] See Nehls, I, 269, 301, 302.—The beetle image reappears in Lawrence's play *David*. King Saul, in a mood of black despair, prophesies that David's God will be devoured by a beetle which hides in the bottomless pit. *The Plays of D. H. Lawrence* (N.D.), p. 261. Since the publication in 1967 of Michael Holroyd's *Lytton Strachey*, with its disclosures of the homosexual relations prevailing in the Keynes group at Cambridge, we are in a better position to understand why Lawrence was so disturbed by his visit there.

[19] *Letters*, I, 360. Cf. *Reflections on the Death of a Porcupine*, pp. 83–84. In a Leconte de Lisle-like passage about baboons and their "unthinkable loins," vultures and other creatures, Lawrence pictures the carrion-eating hyena with the same striking phrase: "his cringing, stricken loins."

dance with joy when I see him rushing down the Gadarene slope of the war." In the Biblical story (about which Gladstone and T. H. Huxley had had their celebrated controversy) a community infected with evil spirits gains some relief by Christ's intervention, the evil spirits being driven out and into a herd of their swine. The swine, like a horde of lemmings, plunge down a slope into the sea and perish.

For Lawrence's purposes in 1916–17, the story of the Gadarene swine was richly suggestive. Not only did it provide one more analogue for the annihilating plunges taking place between the trenches across the Channel but an image suggesting the combination of swinish sensual corruption with a herd madness, an inexplicable propulsion towards self-destruction. The degenerate society, after exhausting all the possibilities of perverse sensuality represented by Loerke, finds its final thrill, its "voluptuous satisfaction"—a phrase describing Gerald's sensations as his fingers tighten on Gudrun's soft throat—in death itself.

In his wartime essay, *The Crown,* Lawrence tried to formulate the connections between what he calls "perversity, degradation and death," especially death in war:

> So that as the sex is exhausted, gradually, a keener desire, the desire for the touch of death follows on . . . Then come . . . fatal wars and revolutions which really create nothing at all, but destroy, and leave emptiness.

Those who prefer to lay the sources of war conveniently at the door of the munitions-makers will derive little satisfaction from Lawrence's recognition of destructive madness: "we go careering down the slope in our voluptuousness of death and horror . . . into oblivion, like Hippolytus trammelled up and borne away in the traces of his maddened horses." [20]

III

The most effective use of the image of the slope occurs during the coming together of Ursula and Birkin on the night before their marriage. After a violent quarrel with her father about her proposed marriage, she arrives at Birkin's cottage in tears:

> He went over to her and kissed her fine, fragile hair, touching her wet cheeks gently.
> "Don't cry," he repeated, "don't cry any more." He held her head close against him, very close and quiet.
> At last she was still. Then she looked up, her eyes wide and frightened. "Don't you want me?" she asked.

[20] *Reflections on the Death of a Porcupine,* pp. 66–67, 80.

"Want you?" His darkened, steady eyes puzzled her and did not give her play.

As in scenes from stories and novels already discussed, the exchange of feelings through the eyes is emphasized, and the ascent from the downward slope culminates in a poignantly rendered coming together:

"Do I look ugly?" she said. And she blew her nose again.
A small smile came round his eyes . . . And he went across to her, and gathered her like a belonging in his arms. She was so tenderly beautiful, he could not bear to see her, he could only bear to hide her against himself. Now, washed all clean by her tears, she was new and frail like a flower just unfolded . . . And he was so old, so steeped in heavy memories. Her soul was new, undefined and glimmering with the unseen. And his soul was dark and gloomy, it had only one grain of living hope, like a grain of mustard seed. But this one living grain in him matched the perfect youth in her.
"I love you," he whispered as he kissed her, and trembled with pure hope, like a man who is born again to a wonderful, lively hope far exceeding the bounds of death. She could not know how much it meant to him, how much he meant by the few words . . . But the passion of gratitude with which he received her into his soul, the extreme, unthinkable gladness of knowing himself living and fit to unite with her, he, who was so nearly dead, who was so near to being *gone with the rest of his race down the slope of mechanical death,* could never be understood by her. He worshipped her as age worships youth, he gloried in her because, in his one grain of faith, he was young as she, he was her proper mate. This marriage with her was his resurrection and his life. [Italics mine.] [360–61]

The poignancy of the release from loneliness is similar to the effect of scenes in "Love Among the Haystacks," *The Rainbow, Lady Chatterley's Lover,* and "The Man Who Died," but perhaps most moving of all in this novel because of the overpowering nature of the destructive rhythms and the variety of ways in which they have been made to sound throughout the action. The hero is not a mere visitor full of righteousness; he is himself a citizen of Sodom, infected with a society's hatreds, degeneracy, and desire for death. Whatever the African statue stood for, as I suggested above, attracts all the characters, even at times Ursula, who usually insisted that she was a "rose of happiness" and not one of the Baudelairian flowers. And for Birkin the attraction had been a powerful one. "You are a devil, you know, really," Ursula says to him early in their relationship. "You want to destroy our hope. You *want* us to be deathly." And later: "You are so *perverse,* so death-eating."

The perversities associated with the statue take in more than being half in love, as Birkin was, with easeful death. What the "further sensual experience" might be which prompted him to his soliloquy, and which he decides to repudiate, has already been indicated. As for the "horror" of homosexuality, there have been readers, beginning with the early reviewers of the novel, who find the "Gladiatorial" and "Man to Man" chapters in this respect obscene. And if Lawrence had included the "Prologue" chapter with which he had originally opened the novel, with its account of Birkin's realization that he likes the bodies of men better than the bodies of women, such readers would have had even more cause for alarm. The problem is extraordinarily complex and (not in the mere squeamish sense) delicate, calling for a nice discrimination between an "abomination" and an ideal relation, a discrimination that some readers may be too impatient to make. In his 1918 essay on Whitman, Lawrence himself struggled to clarify the differentiation which had been assumed in his novel. For having sung of the "love between comrades" Whitman is highly praised by Lawrence as one who had made pioneering efforts on behalf of a great cause. Such a love, provided that it never acts "to destroy marriage" is recommended as healthy and life-giving. If it becomes an alternative to married love instead of a supplement, it is, on the contrary, deathly.[21] The *Blutbrüderschaft* that Birkin wanted to establish with Gerald was supposedly a life-giving relationship not to be confused with the deathly degeneracies evoked in his soliloquy.

With the help of the Whitman essay, this distinction can perhaps be grasped, although as the final page of the novel shows, Ursula herself adamantly refused to grasp it. "I wanted eternal union with a man too: another kind of love," Birkin says wistfully.

"I don't believe it," she said. "It's an obstinacy, a theory, a perversity."

More difficult to grasp, however, is the parallel differentiation between some of the corruptive relations suggested by the statue and the innocence of exploratory relations between men and women as lovers. And here Ursula can, herself, be the spokeswoman for the innocence. At the ski-resort she reflects as she is going to sleep:

> They might do as they liked . . . How could anything that gave one satisfaction be excluded? What was degrading? . . . Why not be bestial, and go the whole round of experience? She exulted in it. [403]

This passage is only slightly veiled and offers few problems. What was puzzling is the earlier scene at an English inn when Ursula discovers in Birkin's body "the source of the deepest life-force."

> She had thought there was no source deeper than the phallic source. And now, behold, from the smitten rock of the man's body, from the

[21] D. H. Lawrence, *The Symbolic Meaning*, ed. Armin Arnold (1962), p. 263.

strange marvellous flanks and thighs, deeper, further in mystery than the phallic source, came the floods of ineffable darkness and ineffable riches. [306]

In 1961, G. Wilson Knight set out to explain what Lawrence was picturing in this curious scene by citing lines from the love poems in which the woman "put her hand on my secret, darkest sources, the darkest outgoings." As might be expected, Knight's explanation prompted an outburst of angry articles in the magazines, most of them concerned with *Lady Chatterley's Lover*. Indeed the novel went on trial, in effect, for a second time. A lawyer, the Warden of All Souls at Oxford, discovered that in one of the several sexual encounters described in that novel, intercourse in the Italian style had been practised.[22] It had also been occasionally practised, it seems, by Will and Anna in *The Rainbow* and by Birkin and Ursula in the scene in the Tyrol referred to above.

For the present discussion I am not going to be concerned with the legal or even the aesthetic aspects of the practice beyond simply endorsing Mark Spilka's comment (made several years before the controversy became prominent) that Lawrence treats it as an act having a limited function which, as a Puritan, he seems to have thought can serve as a kind of "discovery and purification." [23] What is relevant here is not whether some sort of Ovidian *Ars amatoria* could be compiled from Lawrence's writings, but whether the passages cited from *Women in Love* represent a serious artistic blunder on the part of the novelist, creating such a blur that the theme of the novel, and the drama of the hero's development, are both hopelessly obscured. More specifically, if the "dreadful mysteries, far beyond the phallic cult" associated with the beetle-faced statue are represented in one scene as degenerate and in another scene (with only a slight shift in terminology) as redemptive —when Ursula is transfigured by her discovery of a "source deeper than the phallic source"—how is a reader supposed to respond to what seems like a total contradiction?

Of the many critical discussions of *Women in Love,* the only one which I have encountered that even raises some of the questions that I have been trying to grapple with here is that by Eliseo Vivas. Vivas'

---

[22] See John Sparrow in *Encounter* (Feb., 1962), pp. 35–43, and June, 1962, pp. 83–88, and replies by Colin MacInnes and Stephen Potter in *Encounter* (March, 1962), pp. 63–65, 94–96. See also Wilson Knight in *Essays in Criticism* (Oct., 1961), pp. 403–17, and Andrew Shonfield in *Encounter* (Sept., 1961), pp. 63–64, and letter to the editor, *TLS* (August 4, 1961). An earlier controversy provoked by Colin Welch's accusing Lawrence of witchcraft can also be found in *Encounter* (Feb., 1961), pp. 75–79, and March, 1961, pp. 52–55. Also relevant are Middleton Murry's comments in his *Reminiscences of D. H. Lawrence* (1933), pp. 223–27.
[23] Mark Spilka, *The Love Ethic of D. H. Lawrence*, p. 100.

conclusion is that Lawrence introduced a contradiction which is seemingly not resolved, because the novelist has pictured Birkin as rejecting "the African process" and then shown him as, in effect, succumbing to it.[24] On these grounds we might throw up our hands and say of Lawrence himself what Ursula, in a fit of pique, said of Birkin: "He says one thing one day, and another the next—and he always contradicts himself." What may be enjoyed as a colorful trait in a fictional character is not necessarily a commendable asset in the artist who created the fictional character. Fiction can be great when it is tentative and exploratory, making us aware of the puzzling complexities of choice confronting the characters, but if it is merely muddled it will not stand.

As when discussing the cathedral scene in *The Rainbow* I myself suggest again that although Lawrence may be asking too much of us in his account of Birkin's development, the sequence itself is not a muddled one. We are being expected to discriminate between sensual experiences enjoyed by a pair of loving men and women (which are regarded by the novelist as innocently enjoyed) on the one hand, and degenerate indulgences of a society which has cut all connections with spiritual values on the other. Perhaps like the comparable discrimination we were expected to make between a full-fledged homosexual relationship and *Blutbrüderschaft* we may, despite the cluster of horrors associated with the statue, find the distinction too fine, too naïve even, for the stretch of our patience. Yet if we are to understand the development of the characters as well as the social background against which their relations are worked out, the effort to establish the distinction is one worth making. Again, as with the discussion of Whitman, we can derive some help from one of Lawrence's essays. In *Pornography and Obscenity* he writes:

> The sex functions and the excrementory functions in the human body work so close together, yet they are, so to speak, utterly different in direction. Sex is a creative flow, the excrementory flow is towards dissolution, de-creation, if we may use such a word. In the really healthy human being the distinction between the two is instant, our profoundest instincts are perhaps our instincts of opposition between the two flows. But in the degraded human being the deep instincts have gone dead, and then the two flows became identical . . . It happens when the psyche deteriorates, and the profound controlling instincts collapse.[25]

The discriminatory effort required in this instance, it may be added, is called for in many other places of this story, for *Women in Love* is one of the most demanding of novels. The kind of complexities

---

[24] Vivas, *D. H. Lawrence*, pp. 261–67.
[25] *Phoenix*, p. 176.

encountered in discussing the two soliloquies, Birkin's and Gudrun's, which I have been treating expansively here, could be demonstrated again in connection with what Vivas has called the "constitutive" symbols of which the novel is full—the great scene of Birkin stoning the moonlit water for example,[26] or the winter scenes in the mountains culminating in Gerald's confronting another statue, a Tyrolian Christ sticking up out of the snow "under a little sloping hood, at the top of a pole."

What I have been stressing myself is that the complexities derive much of their density from Lawrence's choosing to portray Birkin in particular not as a White Knight, incorrupt and incorruptible, but as a suffering character dramatically involved in extricating himself from a death-loving world to which he is deeply, almost fatally, attracted. Like Conrad in similar presentation of Kurtz and Marlow, Lawrence in this way perhaps doubles the difficulties confronting his readers, but the clear gain in the over-all effectiveness of his novel as a novel is beyond measurement. In a society made up of "a herd of Gadarene swine, rushing possessed to extinction," [27] Gerald Crich is clearly infected with the madness and perishes. Birkin himself is a near casualty. As Wilfred Owen says in his haunting late fragment, *Strange Meeting*: "Foreheads of men have bled where no wounds were." But these affinities (or lack of them) between Birkin and his industrialist friend can be more conveniently developed in a brief *Exeunt* chapter.

[26] Again Vivas' account (pp. 257–61) is especially helpful. For a contrasting interpretation of the scene, see Murray Krieger, *The Tragic Vision* (1960), pp. 37–49.
[27] *Letters*, I, 520.

Suspended Form: Lawrence's Theory of Fiction in *Women in Love*

by Alan Friedman

Consummations are wished for. The formal organization of the eighteenth- and nineteenth-century novel embodied the premise that solutions and resolutions are desirable, that the long fictional disturbance we call the Novel would arrive, after its greatest climax, at an ending that would and could check the foregoing disturbance. But in the twentieth century another assumption about the nature and end of experience slowly came to influence the construction of fiction. The major modern tradition of the novel found energy by opposing a new premise to the old. Novelists created disturbances that ended by remaining still unchecked—in extreme cases, as in the case of D. H. Lawrence, still expanding. In the light of tradition, the shift from a closed to an open or suspended form was a formal insult. But it was more. It was not only an attack on the end of the novel; it was a calculated assault on the ends of experience.

The change was widespread and it was deliberate. In his *Journal of the Counterfeiters* André Gide writes:

> This novel will end sharply, not through exhaustion of the subject, which must give the impression of inexhaustibility, but on the contrary through its expansion and by a sort of blurring of its outline. It must not be neatly rounded off, but rather disperse, disintegrate. . . .

In *The Trial* Franz Kafka comes to

> "A melancholy conclusion," said K. "It turns lying into a universal principle." K. said that with finality, but it was not his final judgment. He was too tired to survey all the conclusions arising from the story. . . .

K. is still wondering at the end of *The Trial*, "Where was the Judge

---

"Suspended Form: Lawrence's Theory of Fiction in Women in Love" by Alan Friedman. This essay was revised especially by Alan Friedman for this collection and includes material from The Turn of the Novel by Alan Friedman (New York: Oxford University Press, *1966*). Copyright © *1966* by Alan Friedman. Reprinted by permission of Alan Friedman.

whom he had never seen?" And at the end of *The Magic Mountain* Thomas Mann gives us Hans Castorp's disappearance on the run through the smoke of a world war, perhaps the only way, and certainly an open way, out of the novel's deliberate dialectic of recurrent impasse.

It is in this spirit that E. M. Forster in *Aspects of the Novel* calls for

> Expansion. That is the idea the novelist must cling to. Not completion. Not rounding off but opening out.

Forster's wish finds itself fulfilled in Lawrence's novels.

Sons and Lovers, The Rainbow, and *Women in Love* have all been accused, even by sympathetic critics, of ending peculiarly. "But the conclusion of the novel," David Daiches observes precisely of *Women in Love,*

> with Gerald dead, Gudrun fascinated by an attractively corrupt German sculptor, and Ursula and Rupert facing each other, is far from embodying a final solution. Rupert demands more than a satisfactory relationship between man and wife, and the novel ends on a question.[1]

One can catch here a note of puzzled uneasiness, not about a novel which does not embody a final solution, but about a novel which is *far* from embodying a final solution. Lawrence's most dedicated champion, F. R. Leavis, has only mild misgivings about the far end of *The Rainbow*. "As for the imperfection of *The Rainbow*," he reassures us,

> the absence of an inevitable close matters, when one sees what the book does, not at all. A more serious criticism, perhaps, bears on the signs of too great a tentativeness in the development and organization of the later part; signs of a growing sense in the writer of an absence of any conclusion in view.[2]

Yet surely one is entitled to suppose a formal connection, a meaningful connection, between a great tentativeness and a final instability. Virginia Woolf, sympathetic but worried, notices that in the world of *Sons and Lovers* the reader

> must hurry on. But to what?
> Probably to some scene which has very little to do with character, with story, with any of the usual resting places, eminences, and consummations of the usual novel. . . . The effect of the book is that stability is never reached.[3]

---

[1] David Daiches, *The Novel and the Modern World,* rev. ed. (Chicago, 1960), pp. 168 f.
[2] F. R. Leavis, *D. H. Lawrence: Novelist* (New York, 1956), p. 172.
[3] Virginia Woolf, "Notes on D. H. Lawrence," in *The Moment and Other Essays* (New York, 1948), p. 96.

Whatever one makes of Paul Morel's return to the glowing town on the last page of his novel, or of Ursula Brangwen's vision of a rainbow on the last page of her novel, or of Rupert Birkin's unfinished wish for the love of another man on the last page of his novel, it is clear that not one of the three books ever reaches formal stability. Lawrence's novels do lack the "consummations of the usual novel." It is even a first principle of form in his fiction that the novel and the novelist should seek to reject, deliberately, disconcertingly, that "final power," in Virginia Woolf's phrase, "that makes things entire in themselves." [4]

The energy of "the wave which cannot halt" on page two of *The Rainbow* and the energy of the incessant guest for the unknown midway through ("She must leap from the known into the unknown. . . . her breast strained as if in bonds") [5] give us the energetic shape not only of Ursula's experience but of her author's sense of form in fiction. The fictional movement which begins on page one by telling us

> There was a look in the eyes of the Brangwens as if they were expecting something unknown, about which they were eager.

gathers for a final leap on the next-to-last page when Ursula rejects Anton Skrebensky:

> He was that which is known. (P. 465.)

The movement is strenuous, even frightening. But the final impulse toward expansion in the finishing of Lawrence's novels cannot be considered an aberration.

Fiction before Lawrence attests chiefly and eloquently to the difficult necessity, the validity and dignity, of achieving a conclusive, resolved experience through the course of life. Lawrence, and modern fiction generally, attests chiefly and as eloquently to the reverse: the difficulty, necessity, validity, and dignity of maintaining through the course of life an unresolved, suspended experience. The roots of this change lie tangled deep in the modern experience. But whatever the causes, older assumptions about character, society, and career gave place to newer ones; the relation of the fictional self to the fictional world was restructured; and in short, readers have for some time been witnessing a mutation in the form of the novel which corresponds to a mutation in the ends of culture. The new form of the novel exposes not only heroes and antiheroes but readers, too, to an unlimited experience. And when it does that most uncompromisingly, it gives us our special

---
[4] *Ibid.*
[5] *The Rainbow*, p. 299. Page references for the *The Rainbow* and *Women in Love* are to the Modern Library editions. Future page references will be incorporated in the text.

sense that in its vision of life something is intangibly but forcefully modern.

It is in these terms—as deliberate suspensions of experience, as unstable form—that the endings of *The Rainbow* and *Women in Love* can best be understood. In both cases the open ending is coherent with the nature and development of experience embodied everywhere else in the novel. Ursula's travels—her transcendence of her own limited self, of the limited world of her provincial childhood, and of the conventional form of life—are projected with complete and explicit consistency in *Women in Love*. Traveling to the Swiss Alps with her husband Rupert Birkin, who remains "unknown" to her and in a satisfying sense unknowable, she finds herself thinking

> of the Marsh, the old, intimate farm-life at Cossethay. My God, how far was she projected from her childhood, how far was she still to go! In one lifetime one travelled through aeons. The great chasm of memory from her childhood in the intimate country surroundings of Cossethay and the Marsh Farm—she remembered the servant Tilly, who used to give her bread and butter sprinkled with brown sugar, in the old living-room where the grandfather clock had two pink roses in a basket painted above the figures on the face—and now when she was traveling into the unknown with Birkin, an utter stranger—was so great, that it seemed she had no identity, that the child she had been, playing in Cossethay churchyard, was a little creature of history, not really herself.
>
> So long as they were moving outwards, she was satisfied. They came to Zurich, then, before very long, ran under the mountains, that were deep in snow. At last she was drawing near. This was the other world now. (Pp. 445 ff.)

The book-long evolution of the relationships among Ursula and Gudrun, Gerald and Birkin—an interweaving of experience which has been called a "fluid, dance-like movement" [6]—mounts towards its crisis in the "other world." We might glance briefly here at the final phrases in the choreography. For Gudrun and Gerald, the gradual drift towards a duel to the death culminates at last, high in the snow, in Gerald's deathgrip on Gudrun's throat. After that, Gudrun packs off to Dresden to enter into a still more sinister dance offstage with the German sculptor Loerke. And Gerald keeps climbing to death until he is finally frozen solid. For Ursula and Birkin, the other two central dancers, the crisis in experience occurs after Gerald's death in a curtain-stopping *pas de deux:* but we will come to that shortly.

It is, in fact, not at all difficult to show that the dance of experience

---

[6] Mark Schorer, "*Women in Love* and Death," in *D. H. Lawrence: A Collection of Critical Essays,* ed. Mark Spilka (Englewood Cliffs, N. J., 1963), p. 56. First published in *The Hudson Review,* VI (Spring, 1953).

in *Women in Love* is left entirely inconclusive, or to show that its ending is left open and expanding. But what is perhaps more interesting to observe is that Lawrence has actually embedded an essay on the theory of fiction within the text of his novel, almost in the manner of Fielding and Gide. That is to say, Lawrence debates how to write a novel, and specifically how to end one, while he writes and ends his novel. Fielding's rather more wide-ranging literary discussion can of course be separated, more or less, from his narrative proper, whereas the notes and plans made in the course of Gide's novel by Gide's Edouard, for a novel to be entitled "The Counterfeiters" can hardly be pried loose from *The Counterfeiters* without emasculating the narrative itself. Lawrence's discussion is still less separable from the body of the novel than Gide's. What Lawrence's characters think and say about themselves and their fate remains (despite what I intend to do to those passages) the very stuff of narrative, not of exposition. Nevertheless, as an examination of the language in which their observations are phrased will at once reveal, their remarks are at the same time calculated theoretical and formal statements.

Consider the following remark by Ursula. In conversation with her sister Gudrun on the opening page of the book, she decides that marriage is "more likely to be the end of experience" than it is to be an experience of any sort. The significance of that remark, made in the first chapter by Ursula, who in the last chapter of her last novel explicitly rejected Skrebensky to prevent the possibility that "her history would be concluded for ever," is worth attention. It is in its own way a consideration and a rejection of the conventional marriage ending. When Ursula marries in this second novel, she will do so in the middle of the story, and she will do so because marriage with Birkin—he and she both say so explicitly (see pp. 360 f., 408, 410 f., 414)—will not constitute an end or an ending in any sense of those words. (Gudrun of course does not marry.)

Less than halfway through the novel and before marrying, Ursula also considers the ending in death. "I am at the end of my line of life" (p. 217), is the way she begins.

> She had travelled all her life long along the line of fulfilment, and it was nearly concluded. She knew all she had to know, she had experienced all she had to experience, she was fulfilled in a kind of bitter ripeness, there remained only to fall from the tree into death. And one must fulfil one's development to the end, must carry the adventure to its conclusion. And the next step was over the border into death. So it was then! There was a certain peace in the knowledge.
>   . . . One can never see beyond the consummation. It is a great and conclusive experience. (P. 217.)

From the terms in which Ursula couches her reflections, it is clear that she analyzes and regards her life as if she were a novelist treating the fiction of her experience.[7]

Ursula of course does not die. She marries Birkin and travels to the continent; and so it turns out to be neither death nor marriage but a trip—traveling—which defines the last section of her history. As she stands with Birkin on the prow of the ship, "the sense of the unrealised world ahead triumphed over everything" (p. 443).

But I am not so much concerned here with the specific ways in which Lawrence achieves his open ending as with his discussion within the novel of the theory of the open conclusion. Observation like those of Ursula's above (Birkin's lengthy speculations in chapter XIX, pp. 289–90, on Gerald's probable end, provide another example) occur in a scattered way here and there through the body of the text.[8] But toward the end they occur (though still covertly) with such concentration that it is not unreasonable to regard the final section of *Women in Love* as a remarkable essay on finality in fiction. The novel does not simply move toward "The End": it talks about itself as it moves there or thereabouts, all the while ringing a variety of changes on the terms "end" and "conclusion." Indeed, the final section becomes in its own way a deliberate *apologia* for what Virginia Woolf called Lawrence's abandonment of "the usual resting places, eminences, and consummations of the usual novel." Only quotation in detail can reveal the elaborateness and self-consciousness of the novel's preoccupation with itself not merely as experience or meaning, but as a form for the achievement of both.

> [Gudrun] wanted to climb the wall of white finality, climb over, into the peaks that sprang up like sharp petals in the heart of the frozen, mysterious navel of the world. She felt that there, . . . among the final cluster of peaks, there, in the unfolded navel of it all, was her consummation. (P. 467.)

> [Gerald] had the faculty of making order out of confusion. Only let him grip hold of a situation, and he would bring to pass an inevitable conclusion. (P. 475.)

> A certain violent sympathy, however, came up in [Gudrun] for this mudchild [Loerke]. There was no going beyond him. (P. 486.)

> "And what *is* the end?" [Gerald] asked.

[7] Compare *The Rainbow*, pp. 456–58.
[8] The theoretical comments on the novel in chapter nine of *Lady Chatterley's Lover* provide another instance in another novel.

Birkin shook his head.
"I've not got there yet, so I don't know. Ask Loerke, he's pretty near." (P. 487.)

[Ursula] felt so doomed up here in the eternal snow, as if there were no beyond. (P. 494.)

"Do you *feel*, Ursula," Gudrun began, rather sceptically, "that you are going-away-for-ever, never-to-return, sort of thing?" (P. 498.)

"There's something final about this. And Gudrun seems like the end, to me," [Gerald said]. (P. 501.)

"Over, is it?" [Gerald said to himself.] "I believe it is over. But it isn't finished. Remember, it isn't finished. We must put some sort of a finish on it. There must be a conclusion, there must be finality." (P. 526.)

All possibility—that was the charm to [Gudrun], the lovely, iridescent, indefinite charm,—pure illusion. All possibility—because death was inevitable, and *nothing* was possible but death.
She did not want things to materialise, to take any definite shape. (P. 533 f.)

"*Wohin?*"
That was the question—*wohin?* Whither? *Wohin?* What a lovely word! [Gudrun] *never* wanted it answered. Let it chime for ever. (P. 536.)

[Gerald] was weak, but he did not want to rest, he wanted to go on and on, to the end. Never again to stay, till he came to the end. . . . (P. 539.)

Birkin tapped and entered [after Gerald's death]. His face was white and expressionless. She knew he knew. He gave her his hand, saying:
"The end of *this* trip, at any rate." (P. 542.)

As readers of the book will recall, and as all of the passages excerpted above clearly suggest, both Gerald and Gudrun do indeed reach a kind of dead end in the novel: Gudrun ends with Loerke, who is the "rock-bottom" of her continuing corruption and whom there is "no going beyond"; and Gerald ends alone among the ice peaks, become "cold, mute Matter" (p. 546). The two characters who have perverted the living mysteries come appropriately to an inevitable conclusion. Their endings are not tapered off: they are simply frozen solid (Gerald) at the very height and buried alive (Gudrun) in the lowest mud (see p. 486) when they have reached the farthest extremities of their narrative motion. (Their ends correspond to two of the circles in Dante's *Inferno,* torments which are equally without end.) Their experience is unresolved, but it is final.

And appropriately, Ursula and Birkin, who in the course of the fiction have gained "faith in the mystery . . . new, deep life-trust" (p. 547), find themselves in a state or, rather, a flight of transcendence in which they can arrive at no possible conclusion. Earlier in the book they do arrive at one of the usual eminences and consummations of fiction. It is rather unusually phrased as a "wonder, the wonder of existing not as oneself, but in a consummation of my being and of her being in a new one, a new paradisal unit regained from the duality" (p. 423). And we duly learn in the next paragraph that "they were married by law on the next day." But in fact Birkin has already warned Ursula (and the reader-critic) that he will not rest content with the ending in marriage.

> "It's the problem I can't solve. I *know* I want a perfect and complete relationship with you: and we've nearly got it—we really have. But beyond that. *Do* I want a real, ultimate relationship with Gerald? Do I want a final, almost extra-human relationship with him—or don't I?
>
> She looked at him for a long time, with strange bright eyes, but she did not answer. (P. 415 f.)

The problem is given as insoluble; and it is phrased as a question which Ursula does not answer.

Given the form for experience toward which, as we have seen, Lawrence has been coherently working, it is therefore appropriate (and not, as has been suggested, a weakness in construction)[9] that the open question should recur in the ending and remain there, crucial and unsolved, after the climax of the book. That ending is even a satisfying one, provided of course that one does not quite unreasonably insist on deriving one's satisfactions only from the fulfilment of expectations and assumptions already perforated and pulverized everywhere in the novel. The entire book—even the very limited number of quotations from it presented above—has made its form evident. The lack of resolution which Lawrence achieves is imperative: the "saved" must end irresolute, only the damned can afford finality.

The climax in experience for Ursula and Birkin, the passage of widest moral and emotional apprehension, occurs in the watch over Gerald's corpse.

> . . . suddenly his heart contracted, his own candle all but fell from his hand, as, with a strange whimpering cry, the tears broke out. He sat down in a chair, shaken by a sudden access. Ursula who had followed him, recoiled aghast from him, as he sat with sunken head and body convulsively shaken, making a strange, horrible sound of tears.

[9] Graham Hough, *The Dark Sun: A Study of D. H. Lawrence* (New York, 1957), p. 85.

> "He should have loved me," he said. "I offered him."
> She, afraid, white, with mute lips answered:
> "What difference would it have made!"
> "It would!" he said. "It would!" (P. 546.)

There is no tapering away, not even after Ursula and Birkin return to England.

> "Aren't I enough for you?" she asked.
> "No," he said. (P. 548.)

The narrative—and Birkin—have already made sufficiently clear that the marriage ending in eternal union is not enough: "to make it complete, really happy, I wanted eternal union with a man too."

> "You can't have [two kinds of love], because it's false, impossible," she said.
> "I don't believe that," he answered.

The End

Thus the book as a whole remains disquietingly—hence satisfyingly—and quite monumentally open after its crises.

A question remains: have we really been looking at a theory of endings in fiction or indeed at a theory of ends in life? The question can be considered in this more general form: can we distinguish at all properly between a theory about life when it is expressed in fiction, and a theory about fiction? Lawrence himself would most probably have rejected altogether the possibility of the distinction. And surely it is right and proper that a novelist should conceive his theory of life in the shape of novels, that he should think in novels when he thinks of life.

> . . . . A more severe,
> More harassing master would extemporize
> Subtler, more urgent proof that the theory
> Of poetry is the theory of life.[10]

In the background of Lawrence's novel we hear Gerald Crich muttering "in a trance" on page five hundred and one, "It's a complete experience. . . . It's not finished—." And we ponder what it is that Birkin has in mind when, after considering all the possible ways in which Gerald might have saved himself from freezing and have gone on to Italy, he admits:

---

[10] Wallace Stevens, "An Ordinary Evening in New Haven," *The Collected Poems of Wallace Stevens* (New York, 1961), p. 486.

He might! And what then? . . . What then? Was it a way out? It was only a way in again. (P. 545.)

Theory of life or theory of the novel: one takes one's choice. But the evidence in *Women in Love* makes it safe to say that Lawrence regarded a conclusive ending as a corruption of the form of life *and* the form of fiction.

Women in Love and the Lawrencean Aesthetic

by David J. Gordon

I

In a well-known letter to Edward Garnett justifying the originality of what was becoming *The Rainbow* and, by extension, *Women in Love,* Lawrence objects to the predictable moral scheme whereby the characterizations of Turgenev, Tolstoi, and Dostoevsky are organized and declares that there is "another ego, according to whose action the individual is unrecognisable." Therefore, he advises Garnett, "don't look for the development of the novel to follow the lines of certain characters: the characters fall into the form of some other rhythmic form."

The letter no doubt claims too much. *Women in Love* owes a manifest debt to such a nineteenth-century tradition, particularly if it includes George Eliot's *Middlemarch*. Its characters take on identity from their relation to a society, however much they excoriate the values of that society or even its existence, and the narrative describes more or less consecutively how they meet and mingle, marry or die. Nevertheless, Lawrence's manifesto is relevant and important for an understanding of his most complex novel. Its distinctive urgency, indicated by the quality of its pervasively heightened rhetoric, leads us beyond the boundaries of the familiarly human toward something more allegorical, ideational, abstract. The swelling up of passage after passage toward symbolic meanings is quite excessive for the purpose of advancing the story. We learn to make sense of these meanings by relating them not only logically and consecutively but also analogically and circuitously. And we learn to accept as trivial the abruptness of transitions and the semi-implausibility of situations, for we expect to be hurried forward toward a kind of meaning that has little to do with realistic social conventions. Lawrence, as the textbooks say, writes a poetic prose—meaning, of course, not a merely florid prose with many

---

This essay was written especially for this anthology. Copyright © 1969 by Prentice-Hall, Inc. All rights reserved.

descriptive passages but a prose that apprehends experience in the more immediate and archaic manner of poetry.

The style of the novel, to be more precise, is a tension of contrary forces: on the one hand an absolutizing imagination which strains against limits ("She felt [that Gerald's passion] would kill her, she was being killed"); on the other, a strong if impatient resistance to absoluteness which causes Lawrence to force in needed qualification, to emphasize the tentativeness of formulations by much repeating of phrases in slightly modified forms, to combine a good deal of colloquialism with his poetic-psychological-metaphysical vocabulary, and to admit that language altogether is an imperfect medium for conveying truth:

> "Why should love be like sleep?" she asked sadly.
> "I don't know. So that it is like death—I *do* want to die from this life—and yet it is more than life itself. One is delivered over like a naked infant from the womb, all the old defences, and the old body gone, and new air around one, that has never been breathed before."
> She listened, making out what he said. She knew, as well as he knew, that words themselves do not convey meaning, that they are but the gestures we make, a dumb show like any other. [178]

Reading *Women in Love* one is both *impressed* by the astonishing plasticity of Lawrence's phrasing and *oppressed* by a certain rhetorical monotony, for the intenser passages narrow repeatedly into either a clinch of rage against bullying will, mechanical abstraction, and bourgeois meanness or a swoon-surge of death and rebirth which almost always suggests sexual intercourse whether the actual subject is the arrival of a carriage, a wrestling match, a kiss, a journey, or an attempted murder.

The form of *Women in Love* can also be described as a tension of opposites: between the "poetic" interest in states and the "novelistic" interest in characters whose destinies we can care about. The novel form, as W. H. Auden observed, does not easily accommodate an interest in states:

> Like Blake, Lawrence was interested not in "individuals" but in "states." In writing about nature or about strangers this does not matter, as these are only experienced as states of being, but it is a serious drawback in writing fiction which cannot avoid the individual and his relations to other individuals over a stretch of time. Lawrence is never at ease when the time is a long one, so that none of his long novels quite succeeds because we get bored with the lack of a character to bind the states together and give them uniqueness.

One solution to the problem that Lawrence adopted in *Women in Love* is simply to compromise with realistic conventions and, despite an aesthetic theory that scorns social identity and predetermined endings, to interest us in his people and their destinies by various traditional means. But this takes us only so far: the pathos of Gerald's death, for example, is subordinate to the more sophisticated interest of its symbolic meaning. Much of the novel, in fact, is organized more or less allegorically: that is, by means of a symbolism energetic enough to dissolve character and event into something like a scheme of ideas.

Deserving of the wide critical attention they have received in this connection are the quasi-parables or set symbolic scenes: such as the scene of Gerald reining his mare in the face of a crossing train, of Birkin stoning and cursing the reflected moon, of Gudrun and Gerald subduing a wild rabbit and exchanging a "hellish recognition." I do not wish to underestimate the value of these scenes, but I became aware on rereading the novel what a relatively small space they occupy, or what a large space is given to the more indefinite and risky symbolism which Lawrence creates by intensifying the language of his psycho-metaphysical encounters to the point that it elaborates the novel's central ideas and images. This more or less spontaneous symbolism is risky because the heightened rhetoric seems hysterical when the dramatic context does not offer strong enough support. Lawrence's obsessive interest in certain ideas—or perhaps his excessively fluid empathy—constitutes a risk in any case because any character who occupies his attention at the moment tends to attract feelings and thoughts that blur with, or belong more fittingly to, those of some other character.

Inconsistencies in the presentation of character and idea can be called a problem of artistic discipline but are perhaps more fundamentally a problem of self-awareness, for we can usually sense their connection to certain half-hidden fears of female domination, homosexuality, and marriage. We will soon consider this problem, but what needs to be said here is that the Lawrencean aesthetic is not necessarily the source of the trouble. Lawrence as critic does put central emphasis on the value of spontaneity, but he also distinguishes the virtue of self-awareness from the vice of self-consciousness and shrewdly sees that an aesthetic which makes a virtue of self-effacement (formulated by Flaubert, Joyce, Eliot, *et al.*) does not guarantee the transcendence of self-consciousness. When an artist effaces himself, "one is far more aware of his interference than when he just goes ahead. . . . Because any self-effacement is self-conscious, and any form of emotional self-consciousness hinders a first-rate artist; though it may help the second-rate." [1] Lawrence's grasp on the strong idea that one gives oneself away in books and should not be afraid to do so (as Gudrun was afraid to do so in her art), that one inevitably writes about oneself

[1] *Phoenix*, p. 248.

even when one succeeds in writing about a shared reality, gave him great freedom of expression. But it is a freedom he abused on the arrogant assumption that he had the power to objectify *every* movement of his own mind.

II

Egoism is probably the most useful single word to describe what Lawrence is seeking to break down in this novel, what he regards as the chief enemy of spontaneous life. But the term will be misleading unless we understand that it signifies a combination of defensive conceit *and* a sense of unworthiness, both of them set over against the wholesome instincts and neither fully conscious. "We are so conceited and so unproud," says Birkin, epitomizing this complex of irrational bigness and littleness.

The struggle against egoism is dramatized primarily by the two major heterosexual relationships, one more or less successful, the other unsuccessful. But to say that Gerald and Gudrun are shown to fail is not to say that they are shown as *meanly* egoistic. Lawrence makes much in the novel of the flux of corruption, the passion for destruction that pervades society although most people are too stubbornly idealistic to recognize that their belief in love is betrayed by their enactment of hate. The decadent sensuality of Gerald and Gudrun is activity "within the ego" rather than against it and so cannot lead to rebirth, but it is passional, authentic activity which shows us what we are, unlike the mean timidities of conventional people. (It is symbolized in the novel by the primitive statuette, which represents according to Birkin "an extreme of physical sensation, beyond mental consciousness.") Gerald and Gudrun are profound, unwilling cynics; they do not believe in a life-giving faith—brotherhood or marriage—and can only resort finally to irony or sentimental illusion. For Gudrun "the last flavor of everything was ironical," and she joins Loerke in a spirit of promiscuous mockery—but they (and Gerald too) want to isolate art, regarding it, sentimentally, as pure. Similarly, Gerald says to the others with a sentimental flourish, "Don't be too hard on poor old England. Though we curse it, we love it really"—but "to Ursula there seemed a fund of cynicism in these words."

Another way of saying all this—and it may help to explain the superiority of *Women in Love* to any of Lawrence's later novels—is that Lawrence has not yet lost the patience or the power to empathize with a tragic character; he is not yet driven so hard by self-repudiation that he must view the undesirable in a purely satirical light. Even Hermione and Loerke, though they are viewed more satirically than the two couples, are Lawrencean aristocrats in that they are free of cupidity and the fear of social convention.

Birkin, of course, comes closest to speaking for Lawrence himself, and it is indicative of Lawrence's effort to be honest with himself that Birkin and his ideas are frequently subjected to criticism by the other characters. But the effort is sometimes crude. Mockery of Birkin is likely to be itself canceled by mockery: as when Halliday and his bohemian cronies are reading Birkin's letter aloud in the Pompadour and are shamed by Gudrun; or when Gerald and Gudrun in Birkin's motorcar are mocking his views on marriage literally behind his back and Birkin begins to feel (with Lawrence evidently wanting us to shift our sympathy to him) a "creeping at the back of his spine." The long haggle between Birkin and Ursula over the meaning of love is apparently supposed to result in some sort of compromise, but it is difficult to see that their final understanding is anything but a capitulation on Ursula's part—or at best a shift of ground from the definition of love to the question of a supplementary male friendship. Lawrence even sets her expounding ideas (about the priority of the individual to love) which she had earlier disputed.

Too often what would seem to belong to the character of Birkin—especially anything to do with fear, weakness, or passivity—is "displaced" onto others. It is Birkin who rebels most passionately against dependence upon a past, but significantly it is Birkin alone of the four principals who is not assigned a background. (Lawrence even deletes mention of his Oxford education and his authorship of brilliant essays in education, indicated in an earlier version of the novel,[2] which would help fill out a certain blankness in our sense of him.) And it is to Ursula that the longest and frankest passage about such dependence is given—although even at that the admission is effectually withdrawn before the passage is concluded:

> She wanted to have no past. . . . She felt that memory was a dirty trick played upon her. . . . What had she to do with parents and antecedents? She knew herself new and unbegotten, she had no father, no mother, no anterior connections. . . . [399–400]

It is Birkin who speaks most pointedly of hating love, sex, marriage, and self, but his frankest statement of this hatred (in the chapter "Man to Man") turns rather quickly into an attack on the clutching woman. And it is difficult not to sense a connection, though Lawrence does not encourage us to do so, between Birkin's various attacks on dominating females and his search (important enough to be given

---

[2] This version, a very interesting document of some twenty pages, given the title "Prologue to *Women in Love*," has recently been published in *Phoenix II*, Warren Roberts and Harry Moore, eds. (New York: The Viking Press, Inc., 1968).

terminal emphasis) for a homosexual bond to supplement marriage. It is Birkin who admits to something "tight and unfree" in himself even in his most Edenic moment with Ursula in Sherwood Forest, but later it is Ursula whose tight lips show that "she could not come forth nakedly to his nakedness." Finally, the usually sensitive and/or awkward Ursula is assigned lines which, even in a novel defiant of social realism, strike us as implausibly tactless, and would make more sense as Birkin's unspoken thoughts (and still more sense, alas, as merely obtrusive expressions of Lawrence's private horror of weakness, injury, illness): when she breaks into a conversation about the subtlety of her sister's sculptures by saying, "I hate subtleties . . . I always think they are a sign of weakness"; when she looks at Gerald's bandaged hand and announces, "I hate people who hurt themselves"; and when she asks the ill Birkin, "illness is so terribly humiliating, don't you think?"

In general Lawrence is more effective and convincing with the man-to-man, woman-to-woman, and woman-to-man encounters than with the man-to-woman ones. The latter are marred by an overready tendency to shift blame and rarefy heterosexuality, which seems to have something to do with an insufficiently admitted inclination toward and fear of homosexuality. Certainly Birkin's "loins" and Gerald's "moulded contours" are far more appreciated by Ursula and Gudrun than are any corresponding physical attributes of the women by the men. And certainly the account in the rejected "Prologue" of Birkin's passionate fascination with male physique in contrast to his mere interest in female faces strikes us as painfully honest and explicit in comparison with Lawrence's treatment of the subject in the completed novel.

The Gerald-Gudrun relationship fares somewhat better artistically than the Birkin-Ursula relationship. Lawrence understands well the profound closeness of hate and love, the excitement and instability of sado-masochistic sexuality, and the connection between sexual and social will to power. Perhaps, however, he invokes the surcharged convulsions and tumescences of Gerald and Gudrun with more intensity and frequency than dramatic need warrants. Moreover, he does not seem quite to see how much their positive feeling for one another appears to be dependent on an initial defiance of parents and bourgeois conventions, as if a certain guilt must be broken down or risen above before desire can be released. Inconsistency of this kind is still more apparent in his treatment of Birkin and Ursula. Birkin *seems* to be rejecting the sensual excesses of Gerald and Gudrun:

> Does there remain to us only the strange, awful afterwards of the knowledge in dissolution, the African knowledge, but different in us, who are blond and blue-eyed from the north? . . . There was another way, the way of freedom. There was the paradisal entry into pure, single being,

the individual soul taking precedence over love and desire for union [while accepting] the obligation of permanent connection with others. [246–47]

But he and Ursula sometimes indulge in a demonic sexuality that is indistinguishable from that of the others—except that, somehow, it is more purifying:

> He had taken her at the roots of her darkness and shame—like a demon, laughing . . . shrugging . . . accepting finally. [296]

> So bestial, they two!—so degraded! She winced. But after all, why not? She exulted as well. . . . She was free, when she knew everything, and no dark shameful things were denied her. [403]

Again, Lawrence seems to ignore the repeated implication that their moments of tenderness, carnal or verbal, are dependent upon an initial defiance.

Gerald Crich is one of the few tragic characters whom Lawrence created, one of the few whom he could esteem and yet destroy. Lawrence as critic hated the tragic figure, the heroic failure like Christ crucified which he interpreted keenly as an image of our love for ourselves in our defeated role.[3] But Gerald's death is presented as a crucifixion and presented with dignity:

> He slithered down a sheer snow slope. . . . There was something standing out of the snow. . . . It was a half-buried crucifix, a little Christ under a sloping hood at the top of a pole. He sheered away. Somebody was going to murder him. He had a great dread of being murdered. . . . Yet why be afraid? It was bound to happen. . . . This was the moment when death was uplifted, and there was no escape.
> Lord Jesus, was it then bound to be—Lord Jesus! He could feel the blow descending. [465]

Elsewhere in the novel Birkin scorns Gerald for his underlying sense of sin and for his lack of faith. But Lawrence is also fairly careful, with both Gerald and Gudrun, to avoid simple scorn. Gerald does impose a mechanical principle in running the mines, but this only satisfied part of his complex, restless nature. His affair with the Virgin-whore Pussum (or Minette) is not mere exhibitionism, as is Halliday's; nor is Gudrun's proclivity for spiteful caricature as superficial as that of Hermione and her guests. Both, especially Gerald, have the courage to quest for deeper, individual fulfillment, which means in part to

---

[3] For fuller discussion of Lawrence and the idea of tragedy, see Chapter IV of my book, *D. H. Lawrence as a Literary Critic* (New Haven: Yale University Press, 1966). See also my article, "Two Anti-Puritan Puritans: Bernard Shaw and D. H. Lawrence," in *The Yale Review* (Autumn, 1966).

recognize their underlying despair. "Things are all right with you then?" asks Birkin, as he and Ursula prepare to leave Innsbruck and their doomed friends. "Gerald screwed up his eyes a little. 'All right? I never know what those common words mean. All right and all wrong, don't they become synonymous somewhere?' "

Perhaps Lawrence is trying to do too much with Gerald. For Gudrun he is the ultimate representative both of masculinity and of the social world of position and power; for Birkin he is, along with Ursula, the irreplaceable member of a necessary new society. But he can hardly satisfy both of them, and he becomes least convincing when Lawrence converts him suddenly toward the end into a sexual failure, changing Gudrun at the same time into a demonic castrator. Tragic characterization splinters here into self-pity and spite but is partially restored when Lawrence rises to the occasion of Gerald's death and at least tells us that Gudrun is herself an outcast, straining for belief beyond the bourgeois world she rejects and unwillingly doomed to "endless unrelief."

Hermione in the first half of the novel and Loerke in the second are mainly satirical characterizations but complex and interesting. Like Gerald and Gudrun they suffer from a profound inner emptiness and cannot achieve life-giving relationship or belief. But whereas Gerald and Gudrun more or less recognize and struggle with their own deficiency, Hermione and Loerke have set their wills against recognizing and thus against wanting to change their state of being. Fundamentally committed to the preservation of existing social forms despite their surface independence of social values, they want the excitement of novelty and new sensation but not real growth, which is painful. Their cynicism is locked into place, as it were, by a corresponding idealism, their materialism by a corresponding sentimentalism. Hermione really believes in "Mammon, the flesh, the devil," even though she grasps with her will at various ideals such as peace, equality, love, or even mentalized versions of sensuality. She is unconsciously hypocritical and, since her "lie" is unreachable, finally insane.

Loerke seems to accept his emptiness and social hatred with disillusioned honesty but he betrays *his* unconscious hypocrisy in his religion of art, a religion that is on the one hand frankly materialistic in its glorification of industry and reverence for the demon of hunger, and that is, on the other hand, overtly sentimental: he and Gudrun "praised the bygone things, they took a sentimental, childish delight in the achieved perfections of the past." They are mockers and like to play at the idea of change but are fatally committed to keeping the shells of their own egos intact. As Lawrence earlier used Birkin to expose the "lie" of Hermione, he uses Ursula in the latter chapters to expose the "lie" of Loerke: "As for your world of art and your world of reality," she tells him, "you have to separate the two, because you can't bear to know what stiff hide-bound brutality you *are* really. . . . The world of art is only the truth about the real world . . . but you are too far gone to see it." (Frank Kermode's objection in *Continuities* then, that Lawrence erred in introducing so major a character as Loerke so late in the story, is partly met by the fact that Loerke has taken over the functions of Hermione, who was conspicuous in the first half of the novel and drops out of the second.)

One must admire Lawrence's brilliant moral passion for bringing the negations in our hearts into the light so that we may be "sound and free." We *are* afraid of change when change means really knowing what we are. But Lawrence's effort is half-undone by his difficulty in bringing what he wanted to be and what he was, "the artist" and "the tale," into balance. The ideal he espouses through Birkin (the ability to love without losing one's integrity) is admirable, but the artist's assault on the obstacles to its fulfillment is often so blindly uncompromising that the tale idealizes again and again something very different: a "will-less" "mindless" "spellbound" "responsibility-free" "passing away," a "lapsing out" in which one is "absolved from actuality."

The more closely one studies *Women in Love,* the more one becomes aware of a rooted, despairing fatalism undermining its moral urgencies. Birkin says, "People only do what they want to do—and what they are capable of doing. If they were capable of anything else, there would be something else." Again, if love really is the greatest good, as people say, "they couldn't help fulfilling it." It is as if Lawrence will tolerate no discrepancy between "ought" and "is" to be bridged perhaps by a sense of humor, and the result is a discrepancy between intention and effect that is not fully within his control, an idealism broken in upon from time to time by a disconcerting cynicism of his own.

The characterization of Gerald is especially pertinent here. Although the moral burden placed upon him would seem to make no sense unless he has some capacity for choice, Lawrence implies that Gerald is damned from the beginning, from birth or earliest childhood. His childhood killing of his brother is regarded by both Birkin and Ursula as no accident but a manifestation of unconscious will. His old nurse tells the sisters that Gerald was so demonic by the age of one-and-a-half that she had to leave the Crich employ: apparently Mrs. Crich, frustrated in her search for individual fulfillment by her husband's devotion to the ideal of Christian charity, had spoiled her infant son. Gerald himself regards his family as hopelessly fated: "Once anything goes wrong, it can never be put right again—not with us. I've noticed it all my life—you can't put a thing right, once it has gone wrong." And Birkin calls Gerald a *born* lover, Gudrun a *born* mistress, as if they are cut off by fate itself from the salvation of marriage.

It is not only the Criches and Gudrun who are absolutely damned. In several striking passages, Birkin, with Lawrence's evident approval, damns absolutely the whole of humanity and places his faith in a metahuman potentiality: e.g. "Let mankind pass away—time it did. The creative utterances will not cease. . . ." But such faith is manifestly self-contradictory since it destroys the believer along with the obstacles to true belief. The quest for a total freedom from anti-instinctual necessity has become a total submission to it.

Philip Rahv shrewdly pointed out how Birkin's idea of true love resembles, in its emphasis on irrevocability, the despised Victorian ideal of marriage.[4] Equally telling is the too close resemblance between his ideal of freedom and his attraction to an authoritarian will to power. Birkin offers a penetrating critique of any democracy which would apply the ideal of equality beyond the superficial purposes of distribution, thus failing to understand that there are no terms of comparison, neither equality nor inequality, between people considered as individualities. Yet Birkin tells us, with no discernible irony on Lawrence's part, that the deepest need of horses and women is to "resign their will to a higher being"; and that Gerald, who was honorable in not wanting to claim social superiority, was stupid in not basing his standard upon "pure being" and claiming "intrinsic personal superiority."

The motive behind such unconscious hypocrisy on Lawrence's own part might be inferred from the novel itself, if one considers the tenor of the death and rebirth metaphor which is so central to its imagery. It is an invaluable metaphor for suggesting various degrees and kinds of psychological and social conversion, but Lawrence's extreme and literal use of it makes us finally sense that its half-hidden purpose is *to deny history*. It does not matter whether the denial is of individual or cultural history since either is meaningless except as fantasy, as psychological defense. The problem of individual history is particularly at issue, however, for Lawrence several times in the novel converts it too quickly into the safer form of a broad social problem, as when Birkin confesses that the "flower" of his soul is a

---

[4] "On Leavis and Lawrence," *New York Review of Books*, XI, No. 5 (Sept. 26, 1968), 65.

"contravened knot" and Ursula is made to reply, "Why is there no flowering, no dignity of human life now?"—a question that Birkin takes up with sudden gusto.

III

There is something heroic in Lawrence's struggle to transcend the dependencies of his past but also something stupid, or at least obstinate, in his refusal to acknowledge and compromise with the humbler layerings of his very complicated mentality. There is also something heroic in his struggle against philosophies that insist on human unworthiness. Like Blake, Lawrence fought hard for the belief that our sense of sin (or sense of guilt) is forged by our minds out of social restraints and, though it does go deep, is totally eradicable. There is no such thing, then, as repression into a permanent unconscious; all fears are capable of becoming conscious. They may be right, though most responsible psychologists today would, I believe, be skeptical, and might inquire how, if Lawrence were right, there could be such a thing as mental illness. The point to make here is that, despite his great courage and intelligence, Lawrence himself could not eliminate from his novel evidence of unconscious fears. The objection is primarily an aesthetic one since the artist has evaded implications raised by words of his own choosing. But we know how searching a writer Lawrence is when even a scrutiny of his inconsistencies leads us into such fundamental issues.

The Discovery of Form

by Julian Moynahan

Women in Love, "a sequel to *The Rainbow* though quite unlike it,"[1] is Lawrence's most fully achieved book, his most difficult, and is one of the half dozen most important novels of the present century. When he had almost completed the final revision in November 1916, Lawrence wrote, "the book frightens me; it is so end-of-the-world," and we know he intended at one point to entitle the novel *Dies Irae*.[2] His description fits the thing done in at least three senses. Like *The Magic Mountain*, *Women in Love* sums up a society which did not survive the first world war and the convulsive revolutionary aftermath of the war. Secondly, it envisions prewar England—and Europe —as though it were already in its death throes. This process of dissolution is represented as going on in society at large, in the sphere of personal relations, in the hearts and souls of individual characters.

Gerald's obsessive tie to Gudrun leads to his own death, but Gerald's efficient reorganization of the Crich family mines has already spelled a kind of death for thousands of workmen by converting them into machine-men. As early as the ninth chapter we hear that Gudrun is "like a new Daphne, turning not into a tree but a machine." At the end, as she prepares to go off with the sculptor Loerke to enjoy a "frictional" relation of witty sensationalism, we understand that the metamorphosis is completed. Since the novel equates the machine principle with death, Gudrun has to be written off for good. Alive with Loerke, who is a kind of vampire figure like Hermione, she is deader than the frozen snowman she has deserted; for even in his dying Gerald retained some vestige of a human quality, if it was only his hysteria.

This process of dissolution is universal in the novel. It is the very form of the society represented and determines the nature of the hu-

---

"The Discovery of Form" by Julian Moynahan. From The Deed of Life: The Novels and Tales of D. H. Lawrence *(Princeton, N. J.: Princeton University Press, 1963, pp. 72–89). Copyright © 1963 by Princeton University Press. Reprinted by permission of Princeton University Press and Oxford University Press.*

[1] Quoted by Richard Aldington in his introduction to the Phoenix edition of *Women in Love* (London: William Heinemann Ltd., 1954), p. vii.
[2] *Letters*, p. 380.

man experience that can take place within the society. Rupert Birkin recognizes that it is going on in himself and coaxes Ursula toward the same self-recognition. He has been more deeply corrupted than she, through his love affair with Hermione, and is therefore more pessimistic than she about the possibilities of escape. Because he "bases his standard of values on pure being"—unlike Gerald, for whom the given societal forms represent ultimate standards—he does not mistake death for life. But he also assumes early on that his generation is involved in a *natural* cycle of destruction preceding a fresh cycle of creation into which neither he nor anyone else can survive:

> "Oh yes, ultimately," he said. "It means a new cycle of creation after —but not for us. If it is the end, then we are the end—fleurs du mal, if you like. If we are fleurs du mal, we are not roses of happiness, and there you are."
> "But I think I am," said Ursula. "I think I am a rose of happiness."
> "Ready-made?" he asked ironically.
> "No—real," she said, hurt.
> "If we are the end, we are not the beginning," he said.
> "Yes, we are," she said. "The beginning comes out of the end."
> "After it, not out of it. After us, not out of us."
> "You are a devil, you know, really," she said. "You want to destroy our hope. You *want* us to be deathly."
> "No," he said. "I only want us to *know* what we are."
> "Ha!" she cried in anger. "You only want us to know death." (p. 165)

Ursula's task is to persuade Birkin to abandon his fatalism so that together they may begin to build life anew. Birkin's task is to make Ursula see that the world as she knows it, and the ideals of that world, are doomed. This means he must teach her to give up her conventional attitude toward love, because insofar as it *is* conventional, that is, conditioned by the present form of society, it is destructive. Also, he must prepare her for eventual flight from the known world. The task is difficult because their departure must literally be a journey into "nowhere," since "everywhere" the cycle of destruction grinds on. Ursula's task is difficult too. Birkin, who is deeply injured "in his soul" as the novel opens, and is almost slain by the frenzied Hermione soon after, is in no optimistic mood. But somehow the couple quarrel each other into a relationship which by the novel's end seems stronger than death.

A third sense in which *Women in Love* is "end-of-the-world" is personal to Lawrence. For Lawrence, as for a great many other European artists of the period, the war came as the greatest shock of his entire life. He loathed the war, utterly disbelieved in the necessity of it, and tended to blame its outbreak on the perverse will of mankind in general. He keeps war out of the book, but cannot keep out the

The Discovery of Form 63

feeling the war had inspired in him. The vision of society-as-death reflects the cycle of destruction through which Europe was passing between 1914 and 1918. Lawrence's revulsion from his fellow man in wartime comes through in Birkin's gloating fantasies of the beauty of a world from which all traces of *homo sapiens* have been eliminated, and in Loerke's nihilistic fantasies of a superbomb that could split the world in two.

Despite these evidences of rage *Women in Love* is not misanthropic *au fond*. Lawrence treats Gerald with tenderness and compassion and all his characters with a characteristic detachment which people who do not know how to read Lawrence invariably take for violent prejudice. Loerke is loathsome, but he is also brave and gifted, just as Gudrun, though perverse, is vivid, beautiful, and self-sufficient. Birkin, who expresses some of Lawrence's cherished ideas, is often ridiculed for his self-consciousness and pedantry; some of the most amusing and happily written scenes are those in which Ursula argues him and his theories into the ground.

Nevertheless, the book demands a toughness and courage from the reader for which it is difficult to think of a parallel. When Birkin and Ursula agree to marry, one of the first things they do is send in written resignations from their jobs. Since Birkin is a school inspector and Ursula a teacher, we must accept the fact that the two liveliest people in a society of the dead and dying abandon the defenseless young to a fate which is destruction. They desert their posts and go off to make a separate peace, like Frederick Henry and Catherine Barclay of *A Farewell to Arms*. Yet that is just the point. Self-sacrifice and devotion to duty are anything but virtues, given the picture of the world Lawrence has created. After all, the zombie-like Hermione yearns to sacrifice herself to Birkin, and one of the first things he tries to teach Ursula is that living selves are *not* to be sacrificed in love, war, work, or whatever. Gerald does his duty as he sees it. In obeying this essential imperative of a ruling class he freezes his own self to death and maims the selves of those who work for him.

Women in Love stands in somewhat the same relation to the real prewar world of England and Europe as one class of Science Fiction novel or Utopian novel stands in relation to actuality. Lawrence detects certain destructive tendencies in his society. He isolates and magnifies these tendencies, predicts their outcome, then merges an essentially apocalyptic vision with the particular segment of historical time he has in hand. The novel compresses reality instead of distorting it. The tone of the opening chapter, describing an upper-class church wedding, is purely Edwardian if not high Victorian. The final chapters, representing in terms of symbolic drama a condition of frozen entropy to which our society has not yet risen, is a prediction of where we may well end up rather than a description of where we were in 1910.

Women in Love is full, perhaps too full, of talk about ideas; but two ideas in particular, one an idea of fate, the other an idea of the fundamental nature of modern Western civilization, emerge as central determining assumptions from which most of the developments of the action stem. The first is adumbrated by Birkin in the second chapter when he is thinking over Gerald's accidental killing of his brother in early childhood.

> What then? Why seek to draw a brand and a curse across the life that had caused the accident? A man can live by accident, and die by accident. Or can he not? Is every man's life subject to pure accident, is it only the race, the genus, the species, that has a universal reference? Or is this not true, is there no such thing as pure accident? Has *everything* that happens a universal significance? Has it? Birkin, pondering as he stood there, had forgotten Mrs. Crich, as she had forgotten him.
>
> He did not believe that there was any such thing as accident. It all hung together, in the deepest sense. (p. 20)

Here Birkin gropes his way to the radical insight that everything that happens in a human career, including chance occurrences, is a revelation of the underlying qualities of being of the man or woman involved. It seems a desperately hard doctrine and not readily defensible. Yet in this particular case Ursula comes to a similar conclusion when in a conversation with Gudrun about the killing she remarks, "I wouldn't pull the trigger of the emptiest gun in the world, not if someone were looking down the barrel. One instinctively doesn't do it."

Ursula's version is easier to accept at once than Birkin's, because she suggests a reason why the accident is not an accident. If one instinctively doesn't do it, then there is some flaw in Gerald's instinctive equipment that enabled him to do it. In fact, Gerald suffers from a defect of "being" which is deadly, and he spreads his deadliness to Gudrun and to his workmen before he is finally disintegrated. Society as it is takes no account of being; it therefore offers Gerald power rather than a cure. Birkin, after diagnosing Gerald's disease, would like to cure him—his absurd proposal of *blutbrüderschaft* and his jiu-jitsu wrestling match with him are efforts in that direction—but in the end he has to flee from the society of which Gerald is the finest flower and master as though from a plague.

How is it that society can accommodate itself to Gerald's defeat, in fact reward him for it, but not to more wholesome beings like Ursula Brangwen and Rupert Birkin? In *The Rainbow* some dialogue was still possible between living selves and societal forms, at least in the pastoral generation to which Tom and Lydia belonged. Why has it ended? The answer lies in the nature of the industrial system, which reaches a final perfection of form under Gerald's management. The following passage, describing the human consequences of the triumph of the machine principle in the Crich family mines, presents Lawrence's full case against the industrial system and against modern society:

> There was a new world, a new order, strict, terrible, inhuman, but satisfying in its very destructiveness. The men were satisfied to belong to the great and wonderful machine, even whilst it destroyed them. It was what they wanted. It was the highest that man had produced, the most wonderful and superhuman. They were exalted by belonging to this great and superhuman system which was beyond feeling or reason, something really godlike. Their hearts died within them, but their souls were satisfied. It was what they wanted. Otherwise Gerald could never have done what he did. He was just ahead of them in giving them what they wanted, this participation in a great and perfect system that subjected life to pure mathematical principles. This was a sort of freedom, the sort they really wanted. It was the first great step in undoing, the first great phase of chaos, the substitution of the mechanical principle for the organic, the destruction of the organic purpose, the organic unity, and the subordination of every organic unit to the great mechanical purpose. It was pure organic disintegration and pure mechanical organization. This is the first and finest state of chaos. (p. 223)

The case is familiar enough and had been made before at least as early as Ruskin. Lawrence's paradox—that the perfection of a mechanical form is chaos—makes perfectly good sense in the light of his concern for the vitality of individual human beings which is destroyed when they subordinate themselves fully to pure mathematical principles of production and distribution. In "The Crown," Lawrence had defined wholeness of being as a conflict. Eliminate the conflict and there is a collapse into chaos. Here the conflict has been resolved into system and order, and it is a chaos from the human standpoint. On the Laurentian view the perfect solution of a given human problem is in fact a dissolution, because it imposes rigid inorganic form on life, and the essence of life is change, variability, pulsation. "The wavering, indistinct, lambent" Birkin is alive by virtue of his "odd mobility and changeableness." His sudden shifts of attitude and feeling, his lapses of taste and logic, protect the life within him. Gerald, who is the soul of good social form, whose ideas are built up logically into lucid formulations, is wholly consistent on his white, gleaming surface but a chaos inside where his feelings are.

The industrial system, like the system of the medieval church to which Will Brangwen had been attracted, solves the problem of living in one mode only. It satisfies the economic needs of men and their hunger for order by arranging their activities according to an intellectualized, simplistic model of human reality. The workmen are satisfied in their souls but their hearts "died within them." The centers of their feeling dry up. They become walking dead like their masters, like the leisured classes which live off the profits of the system (Hermione), like the liberal intellectuals who opt for the social equality of man but accept the system itself (Sir Joshua Malleson), like the bohemians and courtesans infesting the fringes of this humanly decadent society, producing spectacular variants on the universal theme of dissolution (the habitués of the Café Pompadour), like the artists who serve the system by producing art according to the principle that "machinery and the acts of labor are extremely, maddeningly beautiful" (Loerke). In the deepest sense all things hang together, and all classes and groupings of a society whose mystique of production subordinates the organic to the mechanical share the same fate.

Lawrence is careful to avoid giving the impression that the decline of this society could be avoided through a reversion to mindlessness. The point of introducing the pacific carving of the woman in labor and the West African statue of the Negro woman with the elongated neck is to show cultures which declined in a manner parallel to the decline of modern, white industrial society by fulfilling themselves in one mode at the expense of the wholeness of being which constitutes salvation for both selves and societies:

> It must have been thousands of years since her race had died, mystically: that is, since the relation between the senses and the outspoken mind had broken, leaving the experience all in one sort, mystically sensual. Thousands of years ago . . . the goodness, the holiness, the desire for creation and productive happiness must have lapsed, leaving the single impulse for knowledge in one sort, mindless progressive knowledge through the senses, knowledge arrested and ending in the senses, mystic knowledge in disintegration and dissolution. (pp. 245–46)

The point of arrest of Western industrial society is the same, only in the opposite mode. The same relation between mind and feeling has broken; desire for feeling has lapsed, leaving the single impulse to production, disembodied progressive industrial know-how, knowledge arrested in system-making. It is, equally, a knowledge in disintegration and dissolution.

So far *Women in Love* may sound like the sort of fictionalized essay or mere novel of ideas that a Charles Kingsley or an Aldous Huxley might have written. But Lawrence fully translates his criticisms of the character of a civilization into terms of human relationship and human drama. Gerald is the symbol of a social order and Birkin is the prophet of that order's doom; yet both men realize their destinies through personal relationships with women. The two relations, Gerald-Gudrun and Birkin-Ursula, intertwine throughout the book but represent wholly opposed experiences. If the latter is a drama of becoming, the former dramatizes coming apart. Becoming, by definition, has no final conclusion, so that the world of feeling into which Birkin and Ursula move remains as obscure as their ultimate destination after they have left England. Gerald's and Gudrun's drama of disintegration is, by contrast, horrifyingly lucid and moves to a frozen finality. Neither relation is a love affair in the usual sense of the word. Birkin refuses to admit that he wants love—although he comes at last to use that word about himself and Ursula—and Gerald confesses to Gudrun shortly before his death that he cannot love.

Like the other pair, Birkin and Ursula are attracted to each other at first sight. Ursula, just emerging from the state of numbed withdrawal she had endured in the closing pages of *The Rainbow,* swiftly recognizes that Birkin is a man she can love if he will once allow himself to come into focus, and he, as swiftly, realizes that she is the woman with whom he wants to flee the known world and its disease. Setting aside purely novelistic exigencies, their marriage is delayed only because Birkin, who appears to be as deeply injured by his experiences with people when the novel opens as Paul Morel had been at the end of *Sons and Lovers,* needs time to recover health, to work out an adequate theory of relationship, and to train Ursula in the principles of "star-equilibrium" which will determine the relation. There are elements of comedy implicit in this situation of which Lawrence is perfectly well aware, but the problems both people face are serious enough.

At first Ursula wants ordinary romantic love. She assumes that a marriage based on mutual self-sacrifice and mutual absorption, with plenty of sex thrown in, is the proper thing. Birkin, after his disastrous affair with Hermione, knows better. Hermione's will to serve him had proved a will to absorb him, a sort of hideous spiritual cannibalism. When he set his will against hers she had tried to kill him. He has learned the hard way that a will to do loving service can conceal a will to dominate, and treads warily before he involves himself again. If, in the famous chapter called "Moony" (XIX), when he stones the reflected image of the moon on the water, he is trying to break up the image of woman as triple goddess, as some critics have thought, then his action is the height of good sense. The three relations of *Magna Mater* to man are the mother who bears him, the mistress to whom he makes love, and mother earth who takes him inside her upon death. It is sheer folly for a grown man to seek to realize all three relations in one actual woman; since the first relation is entirely regressive, and the third deadly. Hermione, we must assume, had played the first two roles in Birkin's life for a time and aspired as well to the role of goddess of death, when he tried to end their affair.

In the same chapter Birkin suddenly stumbles upon the relation he wants, and it is anything but eccentric. In fact it is classic and normative as a definition of proper marriage.

> There was another way, the way of freedom. There was the paradisal entry into pure, single being, the individual soul taking precedence over love and desire for union, stronger than any pangs of emotion, a lovely state of free proud singleness, which accepted the obligation of the permanent connection with others, and with the other, submits to the yoke and leash of love, but never forfeits its own proud individual singleness, even while it loves and yields. (p. 247)

Put as simply as possible, this idea of the association of man and woman insists that a decent self-respect must balance love and loyalty to the other. It stresses the permanency of the relationship, and concludes that each person must stand on his own feet, regardless of the regressive temptation to let the other person carry him or her throughout life. And by holding the idea of separateness in balance with the idea of union it exactly fulfills the marital ideal already described in *The Rainbow* as well as the requirement for wholeness of being that Lawrence has laid down.

When this idea is finally put to her clearly Ursula cannot help accepting it as a good one. Thus, there is little tension in their love affair of the Tristan and Isolde, Antony and Cleopatra love-death sort. But there are tension and poignancy in the utter contrast this sensible solution makes with the mad world of passion Gerald and Gudrun occupy, and with the civilized world as well. When Birkin and Ursula leave the snow valley they have nothing but their love as a career and a dwelling place. They must, somehow, generate a new world from their nucleus of relatedness, out of the intactness of the single being each possesses. Lawrence is always very moving when he represents his successful lovers flying in the face of civilized society, like Lot's family across the plains from Sodom. In *Women in Love* the account of the train journey from London, across Belgium toward the alpine resort where the Birkins will linger briefly with Gerald and Gudrun, powerfully conveys the pathos of departure toward an unknown future. Ursula remembers her childhood at the Marsh farm and reflects that "in one lifetime one travelled aeons." She sees the man sitting beside her as an utter stranger, but keeps her courage up. Just behind her lie a nasty scene with her father—the hapless Will Brangwen had responded to the news that she wanted to marry Birkin by striking her —and a hurried registry wedding. She and her husband are cut off from everything except each other and the sources of their own beings.

The Discovery of Form

But they are in love and therefore possess, as Birkin once put it, "the freedom together" that wholesome love is.

Gerald Crich, the agonist of *Women in Love,* stands under a kind of triple fatality from the beginning. He is the scion of a family whose vitality is mysteriously defective, who are "curiously bad at living," who "can do things but . . . cannot get on with life at all." Furthermore his nature has been adversely conditioned by the remarkable relation of "mutual interdestructivity" his parents have lived through, which has driven the mother into mental alienation and the father into cancer. Finally, he has his own particular defect, the instinctual flaw that enabled him to play Cain to his brother's Abel. Gerald may also be viewed as a kind of monstrous exaggeration of a characteristic late nineteenth-century English upper-class type, of the man who makes a brilliant administrative career by keeping his feelings under a control so severe that the feelings either turn nasty or die altogether. It is said of Gerald's father that even in the intolerable pain of his final illness he will not face what he actually feels about his wife, his career, about his own death. The same split between a mind which plans and commands and wills and the inner-feeling man is evident in Gerald, making him ideally suited to design a system of production in which living men and women become functions within a mathematical model. Under rigorous suppression Gerald's instinctive responses, already defective by inheritance, conditioning, and fate, turn chaotic. As the essential self begins to disintegrate, the feelings it originates turn destructive and self-destructive. Gerald cannot face the prospect of his own father's death without hysteria because he carries so much death inside him.

He moves in an atmosphere of "essential" death and decay. His early love affair is with the London courtesan Minette, to whom he is attracted by the film of disintegration in her eyes. Water is one of the principal symbols of dissolution in *Women in Love,* and Gerald is intimately associated with that symbol, first as a swimmer (Chapter IV: "Diver"); then in the scene where Gudrun is sketching water plants and he starts up before her "out of the mud," his hand like the stem of one of those plants growing in decay (Chapter X: "Sketchbook"); finally, as the organizer of the water party (Chapter XIV) which ends in the drowning of his sister and a young doctor. Gerald's peripateia comes in that chapter. The cries of the drowning awaken him just as he is on the brink of an experience that might have begun his progress out of his condition of deathliness:

> His mind was almost submerged . . . into the things about him. For he always kept such a keen attentiveness, concentrated and unyielding in himself. Now he had let go, imperceptibly he was melting into oneness with the whole. It was like pure, perfect sleep, his first great sleep of life.

He had been so insistent, so guarded, all his life. But here was sleep, and peace, and perfect lapsing out. (p. 170)

After diving bravely into the dark waters until exhausted, he is brought ashore and says to Gudrun, "If you once die, then when it's over, it's finished. . . . There's room under that water there for thousands." He has seen his own death and is confirmed in the love of death. His life has some months to run, but he is effectively, vitally, finished.

As Birkin shrewdly observes of him early in the novel, Gerald is a potential victim looking to get his throat cut. If Birkin trains Ursula in the career of "star-equilibrium," Gerald trains Gudrun to be his tormenter and slayer. This is not evident at first. When Gudrun watches Gerald hold the terrified mare by means of whip and spur at the gate crossing while the engine passes, her identification with the mare suggests that she will play masochist to his sadist in the ensuing affair. But as time passes the pattern shifts. In the chapter called "Rabbit" (XVIII) they are approximately even, each gloating over the other's wounds. Yet she already harbors in her soul "an unconquerable desire for deep violence against him" and has actually struck him in the face after dancing the highland cattle to madness during the fête at Shortlands. When Gerald comes to her bedroom in Beldover he leaves a trail of clay linking up the grave of his father with the bed of his mistress. It is Gerald's trail, not Gudrun's. By permitting the affair to become the means of Gerald's death she is merely responding to Gerald's deepest will.

The scenes in the snow valley constitute the most brilliant writing that Lawrence ever did, and some of the finest writing in the history of the English novel as well. The valley is a real place and simultaneously a symbol of fate for both Gerald Crich and civilized society. Throughout the novel, his fairness and whiteness have been repeatedly emphasized and associated with the inhuman purity of his social ideas. Here where his vitality is at last to be bled white and empty of Gudrun's hatred, the mathematically perfect forms of snow flakes, composing a chaos of white, mock him and his concepts of fulfillment. It is a world all in one mode, a world without conflict or relief. Gerald as skier, as "snow-demon" is perfectly adapted to it and finally fuses with it when his being comes crashing down "in sheer nothingness" after Gudrun removes the last prop.

By a wonderful shift of emphasis, Lawrence wins for Gerald at the end our deepest sympathies. This is partly achieved through the sheer beauty of the descriptions of him in his isolation, as in the account of his climb upward after he has assaulted Loerke and Gudrun, or in the following paragraph from a few pages before that scene:

So he came down reluctantly, snow-burned, snow-estranged, to the house in the hollow, between the knuckles of the mountain-tops. He saw its lights shining yellow, and he held back, wishing he need not go in to confront those people, to hear the turmoil of voices and to feel the confusion of other presences. He was isolated as if there were a vacuum round his heart, or a sheath of pure ice. (p. 452)

But it is also partly done through the force of contrast between such descriptions and the accounts given of the revolting intimacies newly established between Loerke and Gudrun:

> Their whole correspondence was in a strange, barely comprehensible suggestivity, they kindled themselves at the subtle lust of the Egyptians or the Mexicans. The whole game was one of subtle inter-suggestivity, and they wanted to keep it on the plane of suggestion. From their verbal and physical nuances they got the highest satisfaction in the nerves, from a queer interchange of half-suggested ideas, looks, expressions, gestures. (p. 439)

As is said, it is all suggestivity, and the suggestion here is that we are looking at a couple of robotic insects with exposed ganglia of fine wire consciously parodying human communication.

Given the choice the reader dies imaginatively with Gerald rather than make a threesome with the above creatures. Although Gudrun sees him finally as a boringly complex piece of machinery we see him as a man in the extremity and loneliness of his suffering. When Birkin sits grieving over Gerald's frozen body he wonders whether he had perished in the attempt to climb beyond the snows. If he had reached the crest he might have been able to descend into warm fertile valleys to the south. But then Birkin reflects, "Was it a way out. It was only a way in again." There is no escape. The snow of abstraction lies everywhere in the civilized world. Once a man or a society loses touch with its own deepest sources of being there is no way back. On the last page, Birkin permits himself the sentimental luxury of imagining that he could have saved Gerald by loving him in a union as eternal as his union with Ursula. But she is there at his elbow, thank God, to remind him with characteristic, Friedalike forthrightness that "you can't have it, because it's false, impossible." On that authoritative note they resume their journey into nowhere.

Women in Love is Lawrence's most perfectly integrated study of disintegration. His living selves are fully involved with a milieu thickly rendered and chillingly contemporary. If Lawrence's enterprise after *Sons and Lovers* had been to submit to the anguish of combining the living self with the shell of historical and social actuality his submission in his fifth novel has been complete. Unlike the dimly projected pastoral generations of the earlier Brangwens, who "held life between the grip of their knees," the heroes and heroines of *Women in Love* live close to the sick heart of a doomed civilization and are implicated in its final illness. The principal statement the novel makes is a deeply pessimistic one. It says that a living man or woman who embraces the social destiny offered by industrial Western society in the early twentieth century embraces his own dying. The anguish of combining has become a death anguish.

By contrast, *The Rainbow* is a very hopeful book. In that novel Lawrence could still believe that "the sordid people who crept hardscaled and separate on the face of the world's corruption were living still," and "would issue to a new germination." This faith rested in turn on a deeper faith in unknowable forces of life which might, upon occasion, seize hold of individuals, drawing them out of their ordinary daytime roles and attitudes and restoring them to themselves, provided they had the courage to respond to the call and move under the shelter of the rainbow. The world war killed that faith in Lawrence; not his faith in life but his belief that either the ordinary people who put up with the values of modern society, or the privileged people who had made a conscious commitment to those values would remain alive in the "vital" sense. Nor could he believe any longer that exceptionally lively people might be able to alter that society from within. Early in *Women in Love* Birkin tells Gerald that people must either break up the present system or shrivel within it. By the end he realizes that the only breaking possible is to break and run for his life.

Women in Love, then, completes an entire cycle in the development of Lawrence's thinking and feeling as a novelist. Over a period of seven years he had learned how to construct a dazzlingly original narrative form through which "profound intuitions of life" could be brought to confront the systems of custom and convention, habit and law, work and art, thought and emotion determining the nature of social existence. But this lucid confrontation showed him only that there was no longer any common ground where life and history could meet, mingle, and enhance each other. In not one of the five novels he had left to write appears a single character like the young Ursula of *The Rainbow,* or Paul Morel, characters who run into the world with open arms and with the illusion that the societies into which they have been born can provide the conditions of vital freedom they seek.

No Man's Land

by Mark Spilka

I

Lawrence belongs to that school of writers whose work is often more explorative, more interrogative, than affirmative.[1] His function is to ask new questions, to confront us with new values and inescapable contradictions—or in his own words, to "lead into new places the flow of our sympathetic consciousness, and [to] lead our sympathy away in recoil from things gone dead." Thus he shows us Paul Morel, at the end of *Sons and Lovers,* stepping out quickly in a new direction, away from his three discarded loves; or Ursula Brangwen, in *The Rainbow,* facing that radiant arch expectantly, her soul new-born, her old selves shed behind her like so many wrinkled skins;—and now, in *Women in Love,* he gives us Rupert Birkin, lopped and bound in a marriage which gives him peace but already pulls too tightly on his freedom to develop. Birkin is no sooner married, for example, than he begins to expound to Gerald Crich on the repulsive nature of marriage in the old sense: "It's a sort of tacit hunting in couples: the world all in couples, each couple in its own little house, watching its own little interests and stewing in its own little privacy—it's the most

---

"No Man's Land" by Mark Spilka. From The Love Ethic of D. H. Lawrence *(Bloomington, Indiana: Indiana University Press, 1955), pp. 148–73, in abridged form. Copyright © 1955 by Indiana University Press. Reprinted by permission of Indiana University Press and Dennis Dobson, Ltd. [Throughout this selection, the page references are to the Modern Library edition of* Women in Love.—ED.]

[1] As André Gide points out, Dostoievsky is another writer who poses rather than resolves some of the more difficult problems which confront him. Gide also traces part of Dostoievsky's cool reception in France to the presence of unresolved elements in his work, and cites this as a common hazard for the interrogative writer:

> The public is but ill-pacified by the author who does not come to a strikingly evident solution. In its eyes, it is the sin of uncertainty, indolence of mind, lukewarmness of convictions. And most often, having little liking for intelligence, the public gauges the strength of a conviction by naught but the violence, persistence, and uniformity of the affirmation. (*Dostoievsky,* [Norfolk, Conn. 1949] p. 45)

repulsive thing on earth." Gerald promptly agrees, and the two men search for a more expansive way of life:

> "You've got to take down the love-and-marriage ideal from its pedestal. We want something broader. I believe in the *additional* perfect relationship between man and man—additional to marriage."
> "I can never see how they can be the same," said Gerald.
> "Not the same—but equally important, equally creative, equally sacred, if you like."
> Gerald moved uneasily. "You know, I can't feel that," said he. "Surely there can never be anything as strong between man and man as sex love is between man and woman. Nature doesn't provide the basis."
> "Well, of course, I think she does. And I don't think we shall ever be happy till we establish ourselves on this basis. You've got to get rid of the *exclusiveness* of married love. And you've got to admit the unadmitted love of man for man. It makes for a greater freedom for everybody, a greater power of individuality both in men and women."
> "I know," said Gerald, "you believe something like that. Only I can't *feel* it, you see." He put his hand on Birkin's arm, with a sort of deprecating affection. And he smiled as if triumphantly. (P. 403.)

Gerald's triumphant smile coincides, I think, with our own. We find no place, in our society, for that "unadmitted love of man for man" which Lawrence tried to project throughout his writings. And so we tend to explain the male-love theme in his works on personal or psychological grounds: hence Harry Moore examines the possibility of homosexuality, and then discards it; or he describes the wrestling bout in *Women in Love* as a form of athletic mysticism, and then suggests—"only as a possibility"—that Lawrence was merely trying to identify his personal frailness, in such chapters, with the hero's physical strength (*Life and Works,* pp. 165–66). Perhaps he was. But with one or two exceptions, the friendship scenes in other books do not involve athletics, so that argument falls through on the simple grounds of logic. As for homosexuality (which Moore discounts), the plain fact is that Lawrence was aware of it, and that he rejected it himself as mechanistic and destructive.[2]

Actually, it is a question here of values, and of emotional possibilities, rather than personal failings: we cannot "psychologize" the problem away; we have to face it in terms of the gaps and failures in modern thought itself. For if other cultures than our own have struggled with the friendship problem (the Greeks, the Elizabethans,

---

[2] Witness his handling of Ursula's lesbian affair in *The Rainbow,* and of Loerke's implied affairs in *Women in Love.* His objections to such unions were based, I think, on two distinct beliefs: (1) that men and women must be singled out into pure malehood and pure femalehood; and (2) that homosexual love, like oedipal love, is mechanistic and obsessive—an imposition from without, and therefore a sin against spontaneous life.

the old Germanic tribes, the medieval knights), today we largely deny that such a problem exists. Apparently, we see a kind of no man's land between the casual and the homosexual liaison—and if Lawrence has been foolish enough to inhabit it, that is largely his affair. But let us see, at the least, how much of the forbidden ground he has explored, and with what success, if any.

II

The major expression of the brotherhood theme occurs in *Women in Love*, but a later story, "The Blind Man," may serve here as a short and simple introduction to Lawrence's position. As you may remember, the "blind man," Maurice Pervin, is caught and held within a state of blood-prescience as the story opens. He has enjoyed the rich sensual consummation with his wife, but somehow the experience has proved inadequate. Occasionally, a terrible weariness, a sense of being closed in and swamped with darkness, overwhelms them both. Isabel nearly screams with the strain; she seeks out friends for comfort, but finds them shallow and impertinent in the face of the rich, dark world she shares with her husband. Maurice too is seized with fits of depression, for at times his sensual flow is checked and thrown back, so that a kind of "shattered chaos" occurs within his blood. In the end, however, his energies are aligned and utilized through the friendship rite with Isabel's cousin, the intellectual neuter, Bertie Reid. To repeat only the crucial passage: the two men are talking together in the barn, when Pervin suddenly asks the bachelor lawyer if he may touch him; Bertie complies, and Maurice covers his face, shoulder, and arm with his sensitive fingers, and then asks him to touch his own blind eyes; again Bertie complies—

> He lifted his hand, and laid the fingers on the scar, on the scarred eyes. Maurice suddenly covered them with his own hand, pressed the fingers of the other man upon his disfigured eye-sockets, trembling in every fibre, and rocking slightly, slowly, from side to side. He remained thus for a minute or more, whilst Bertie stood as if in a swoon, unconscious, imprisoned.
> Then suddenly Maurice removed the hand of the other man from his brow, and stood holding it in his own.
> "Oh, my God," he said, "we shall know each other now, shan't we? We shall know each other now." (*The Portable D. H. Lawrence*, p. 103.)

Yet as Maurice overflows "with hot, poignant love," Bertie shrinks back, afraid for his life. And when both return to Isabel: "He could not bear it that he had been touched by the blind man, his insane reserve broken in. He was like a mollusc whose shell is broken." On the other hand, Maurice now stands before his wife, feet apart, "like a strange colossus": "We've become friends," he shouts, and though Isabel's gaze turns, painfully, on the haggard, broken lawyer, she replies, "You'll be happier now, dear." A path, a way out of the darkness has just been opened up for them, then quickly and ironically shut off by Bertie's fear of close, passionate friendship. Yet the human possibility is also clearly there: before this experience, Maurice had seemed strong-blooded and healthy to Isabel, but at the same time, cancelled out; now a new world has been revealed to him, beyond the binding intimacy of marriage and the obvious limitations of a single form of consciousness.

Clearly this is the primary function of male friendship in Lawrence's world: the step beyond marriage which makes marriage possible, the break-through to a fuller life which Lawrence tried to project, in a dozen different ways, in all his novels. This is the first important thing to remember, at any rate, when considering the friendship theme in *Women in Love*.

In the second chapter of that novel, there is a sharp quarrel between Rupert Birkin and his friend, Gerald Crich. Then the two men part with casual unconcern, and each of them suppresses his strange, burning attraction towards the other. Their friendship takes a sharp upswing, however, when Gerald's sister Diana drowns, and Birkin tries (unsuccessfully) to draw him away from the dreadful scene. In the stress of the moment, Gerald confesses that he would rather chat with Birkin than do anything else: "You mean a lot to me, Rupert, more than you know." Later, when Birkin becomes ill, Gerald does visit him, and sits indulgently by his bed, musing, as they talk, that the quick, slim man beside him seems too detached for any depth of friendship. Birkin's thoughts run on opposite lines: he suddenly sees his lifelong need "to love a man purely and fully," and so he tosses forth a first crude version of *Blutbrüderschaft:*

"You know how the old German knights used to swear a Blutbruderschaft," he said to Gerald, with quite a new happy activity in his eyes.
"Make a little wound in their arms, and rub each other's blood into the cut?" said Gerald.
"Yes—and swear to be true to each other, of one blood, all their lives. That is what we ought to do. No wounds, that is obsolete. But we ought to swear to love each other, you and I, implicitly, and perfectly, finally, without any possibility of going back on it." . . .
Birkin sought hard to express himself. But Gerald hardly listened. His face shone with a certain luminous pleasure. He was pleased. But he kept his reserve. He held himself back.

"Shall we swear to each other, one day?" said Birkin, putting out his hand towards Gerald.

Gerald just touched the extended fine, living hand, as if withheld and afraid.

"We'll leave it till I understand it better," he said, in a voice of excuse.

Birkin watched him. A little sharp disappointment, perhaps a touch of contempt came into his heart.

"Yes," he said. "You must tell me what you think, later. You know what I mean? No sloppy emotionalism. An impersonal union that leaves one free." (P. 235.)

After this conversation, the problem drops to the background and the two men go their separate ways. Crich plunges back into business and devotes his energies to the great industrial system he wants to establish; he also makes his first advances toward Ursula Brangwen's sister, Gudrun. Birkin leaves the south of France, returns, and finally comes to closer terms with Ursula herself. But when his hasty proposal ends in fiasco, he walks furiously away from the Brangwen home, straight towards Gerald Crich at Shortlands. He finds Crich restless and irritable with his own emptiness, and therefore glad enough to see him, and, as an antidote to boredom, equally glad to learn the rudiments of jiu-jitsu. The famous wrestling scene follows, Gerald pitting his powerful mechanical strength against Birkin's more elusive and organic energies:

> So the two men entwined and wrestled with each other, working nearer and nearer. Both were white and clear, but Gerald flushed smart red where he was touched, and Birkin remained white and tense. He seemed to penetrate into Gerald's more solid, more diffuse bulk, to interfuse his body through the body of the other, as if to bring it subtly into subjection, always seizing with some rapid necromantic foreknowledge every motion of the other flesh, converting and counteracting it, playing upon the limbs and trunk of Gerald like some hard wind. It was as if Birkin's whole physical intelligence interpenetrated into Gerald's body, as if his fine sublimated energy entered into the flesh of the fuller man, like some potency, casting a fine net, a prison, through the muscles into the very depths of Gerald's physical being.
>
> So they wrestled swiftly, rapturously, intent and mindless at last, two essential white figures working into a tighter closer oneness of struggle, with a strange, octopus-like knotting and flashing of limbs in the subdued light of the room; a tense white knot of flesh gripped in silence between the walls of old brown books. Now and again came a sharp gasp of breath, or a sound like a sigh, then the rapid thudding of movement on the thickly-carpeted floor, then the strange sound of flesh escaping under flesh. Often, in the white interlaced knot of violent living being that swayed silently, there was no head to be seen, only the swift, tight limbs, the solid white backs, the physical junction of

two bodies clinched into oneness. Then would appear the gleaming, ruffled head of Gerald, as the struggle changed, then for a moment the dun-coloured, shadow-like head of the other man would lift up from the conflict, the eyes wide and dreadful and sightless. (Pp. 307–308.)

As the two fall back exhausted, Birkin slips off toward unconsciousness, then rouses to the terrible hammer-stroke of his heart. Gerald too is dimly unconscious, but when Birkin attempts to steady himself their hands accidentally touch: "And Gerald's hand closed warm and sudden over Birkin's, they remained exhausted and breathless, the one hand clasped closely over the other." Then the two slip back to normal consciousness, and Birkin marks out the significance of their experience: "We are mentally, spiritually intimate, therefore we should be more or less physically intimate too—it is more whole"; "I think also that you are beautiful . . . and that is enjoyable too. One should enjoy what is given"; "At any rate, one feels freer and more open now—and that is what we want." This is the *Blutbrüderschaft,* then, which Birkin has been seeking, for the aim here is not sexual gratification (most critics agree on this) but the consummation of friendship.[3] The question remains, of course: just what significance does Lawrence attach to such consummation? My own interpretation follows.

[3] Harry Moore points out (not quite correctly) that "none of these scenes suggests any form of sexual gratification." He also shows that John Middleton Murry, the chief source for Gerald Crich, did not accuse Lawrence of "what is generally understood by the word homosexuality," and that other critics and biographers, friendly or hostile, generally concur on this point (*Life and Works,* pp. 165–66). Several of these critics have argued, however, that Lawrence proffers another and more innocent brand of homosexuality, which seems to correspond with "the bisexuality of our own infant pasts" (*e.g.,* Diana Trilling, *The Portable D. H. Lawrence,* p. 22). I believe there is one genuine example of this sort of experience in Lawrence's first novel, *The White Peacock,* as George Saxton gives Cyril Beardsall a rubdown after a short swim:

> He saw that I had forgotten to continue my rubbing, and laughing he took hold of me and began to rub me briskly, as if I were a child, or rather, a woman he loved and did not fear. I left myself quite limply in his hands, and, to get a better grip of me, he put his arms round me and pressed me against him, and the sweetness of the touch of our naked bodies one against the other was superb. It satisfied in some measure the vague, indecipherable yearning of my soul; and it was the same with him. When he had rubbed me all warm, he let me go, and we looked at each other with eyes of still laughter, and our love was perfect for a moment, more perfect than any love I have known since, either for man or woman. (P. 248.)

But after *The White Peacock,* Lawrence seems to understand the direction of such contacts, and he rejects them. In *The Rainbow,* for example, the affair between Ursula Brangwen and Winifred Inger begins with a kind of innocent voluptuousness, but gradually proves nauseous and degrading. Significantly enough, it also centers around a series of swimming scenes—which makes the change in Lawrence's thought seem all the more conscious and obvious.

First of all, we have just witnessed a spontaneous rite or ceremony between Birkin and Crich. If the terms "spontaneous" and "rite" seem contradictory, please remember that the essence of *any* religious rite is communion, contact, or rapport between the performers and their god or gods. And for Lawrence the life-flow itself is sacred, so that the flow between Birkin and Gerald becomes a religious pledge or vow, a unique and binding experience which stems quite naturally from their separate emotional predicaments and their mutual love.

* * *

By physical love Lawrence means something other than homosexuality. Indeed, he makes the point, in *Fantasia of the Unconscious*, that male relations involve the upper, spiritual poles of consciousness, instead of the lower sexual poles:

> Is this new polarity, this new circuit of passion between comrades and co-workers, is this also sexual? It is a vivid circuit of polarized passion. Is it hence sex?
> It is not. Because what are the poles of positive connection?—the upper, busy poles. What is the dynamic contact?—a unison in spirit, in understanding, and a pure commingling in one great *work*. A mingling of the individual passion into one great *purpose*. . . . Knowing what sex is, can we call this other also sex? We cannot. . . . It is a great motion in the opposite direction. (P. 151.)

This tends to explain, I think, why Pervin is attracted to an intellectual in "The Blind Man," or why Birkin likes an industrialist in *Women in Love:* for Laurentian brotherhood seems aimed, from the first, at "a unison in spirit, in understanding, and a pure commingling in one great *work*."

Yet the sensual element is also present from the first. To explain it, we must turn to the Laurentian concepts of "touch" and "warmth" in human relationships, for the two concepts are closely connected. Thus touch is an emotional, not merely a sensual experience for Lawrence; and even as a sensual experience, *per se,* touch is not necessarily sexual. Think back, in both respects, to the episode in *Sons and Lovers,* when Paul Morel falls sick and his mother sleeps with him at night: at the height of his fever she clasps him to her breast, and the sensual contact helps to cure him.[4] The scene here is

---

[4] For a further example of the "healing powers" of touch, take the completely impersonal scene in *The Lost Girl*, when Arthur Witham hurts his leg while working in the organ loft. Alvina Houghton rushes up from the chapel at the sound of the accident, and examines the wound:

> She put her fingers over the bone, over his stocking, to feel if there was any fracture. Immediately her fingers were wet with blood. Then he did a curious

based upon a sensual expression of love (Paul "realizes" his mother), but not a sexual one. And the same holds true for the sensual contacts which we have just examined, between man and man. As Mellors puts it in *Lady Chatterley's Lover,* "I stand for the touch of bodily awareness between human beings . . . and the touch of tenderness"; as for sex, it is only "the closest of all touch." What Mellors constructs here, in effect, is a scale of sensuality, with physical contact between human beings as the basic experience, and with heterosexual love at the farthest range of the sensual scale: thus other forms of contact, between man and man, woman and woman, or parent and child, can also give valid expression to other, less intimate forms of love.[5]

As we draw these various strands of thought together, the wrestling bout in *Women in Love* begins to take on proper meaning: first of all, it functions as part of a general step beyond marriage to some further living relationship; second, it functions as the spontaneous pledge to keep that relationship alive; and third, it involves an actual physical communion, between self and self, or soul and soul, and therefore functions as a mutual realization of the beloved. One can legitimately protest, of course, that the scene at hand goes far beyond these functions, and that Lawrence has blown it up out of all proportion to man's actual experience—that he has overstressed, in other words, man's capacity for physical, nonsexual communion with his fellow man, and has therefore left himself exposed to honest (and dishonest) criticism. But he has only done so as part of a more general attempt to place *Blutbrüderschaft* itself upon an ideal pedestal—and

---

thing. With both his hands he pressed her hand down over his wounded leg, pressed it with all his might, as if her hand were a plaster. For some moments he sat pressing her hand over his broken skin, completely oblivious, as some people are when they have had a shock and a hurt, intense on one point of consciousness only, and for the rest unconscious.

Then he began to come to himself. The pain modified itself. (P. 88.)

[5] There is, however, an element of "sexual sympathy" in all these forms of love. The men in Lawrence's world are drawn together, for example, by a certain amount of fellow-feeling over their common mistreatment at the hands of women. As Lawrence explains it in one of the late essays:

. . . this silent sympathy is utterly different from desire or anything rampant or lurid. . . . it is just a form of warmheartedness and compassionateness, the most natural life-flow in the world. . . .

And it is this that I want to restore into life: just the natural warm flow of common sympathy between man and man, man and woman. . . . It is the most important thing just now, this gentle physical awareness. It keeps us tender and alive at a moment when the great danger is to go brittle, hard, and in some way dead.

Accept the sexual, physical being of yourself, and of every other creature. Don't be afraid of it. (*Sex, Literature, and Censorship,* pp. 66–67.)

even here he has incorporated his fault into the very body of his work, and has made it part of a *problem posed,* rather than a problem solved. Birkin himself, for example, is scarcely convinced of the final validity of *Blutbrüderschaft:* "I *know* I want a perfect and complete relationship with you," he tells his wife. "But beyond that. *Do* I want a real, ultimate relationship with Gerald? . . . or don't I?" This question is partially answered, I think, by the total failure of the *Blutbrüderschaft* to take hold, and by Ursula's final pointed criticism:

"Why aren't I enough?" she said. "You are enough for me. I don't want anybody else but you. Why isn't it the same with you?"

"Having you, I can live all my life without anybody else, any other sheer intimacy. But to make it complete, really happy, I wanted eternal union with a man too: another kind of love," he said.

"I don't believe it," she said. "It's an obstinacy, a theory, a perversity. . . . You can't have two kinds of love. Why should you!"

"It seems as if I can't," he said. "Yet I wanted it."

"You can't have it, because it's false, impossible," she said.

"I don't believe that," he answered.

The book ends on this stubborn note, with Birkin's brotherhood scheme exploded in fact and theory: the concept of twin loves proves ephemeral, that is, within the fictional testing vat, and Ursula's pointed question—"Why should you?"—remains unanswered. But a decided residue of truth is left over, and Birkin echoes this in his final words. If the love of man for man can never function as a perfect parallel to married love, the question still remains—how does it function? For Birkin's insistence that Gerald should have loved him—that it would have made some difference if he did—is borne out "dramatically" in the book. As Lawrence tells us, marriage would have been a hoax for Gerald, until he achieved some pure relationship with another human-being: "If he pledged himself with the man he would later be able to pledge himself with the woman: not merely in legal marriage, but in absolute mystic marriage"—or star-equilibrium. And indeed, the only point in the book at which Gerald is set free, in perfect balance with another human being, occurs just after the wrestling bout with Birkin. Had the pledge between them held, Crich might have received some badly needed nurturing of the soul. Then too, his warm, vivid chats with Birkin, taken seriously, might well have cleared away that basic mental confusion which thwarted his will to live. But Gerald had no respect for Birkin's notions: his mind was bound by convention, his will was bent toward self-annihilation, and so, as the omen of "Northern ice-destruction," he chose to break himself in the struggle with Gudrun Brangwen.

III

So the first sortie outward from the narrow circle of marriage ends in failure for Birkin—and death for Gerald Crich. But at the same time, the possibility of some kind of brotherhood is established. In the novels that follow, Lawrence reworks this possibility along wholly different lines, scrapping brotherhood *per se* for the lordship principle, and moving much more clearly into the realm of purposive (and spiritual) endeavor. Thus Lilly, the Lawrence-figure in *Aaron's Rod*, tells Aaron Sisson to find himself a leader:

> "All men say, they want a leader. Then let them in their souls *submit* to some greater soul than theirs. . . . You, Aaron, you too have the need to submit. You, too, have the need livingly to yield to a more heroic soul, to give yourself. You know you have. And you know it isn't love. It is life-submission. And you know it. But you kick against the pricks. And perhaps you'd rather die than yield. And so, die you must. It is your affair."
>
> There was a long pause. Then Aaron looked up into Lilly's face. It was dark and remote-seeming. It was like a Byzantine eikon at the moment.
>
> "And whom shall I submit to?" he said.
>
> "Your soul will tell you," replied the other.

The book ends on this cryptic note, but the theme is picked up and amplified in Lawrence's next novel, *Kangaroo*, as Somers, the wandering writer, specifically rejects the old ideal of brotherly affection:

> All his life he had cherished a beloved ideal of friendship—David and Jonathan. And now, when true and good friends offered, he found he simply could not commit himself, even to simple friendship. The whole trend of this affection, this mingling, this intimacy, this truly beautiful love, he found his soul just set against it . . . he didn't want it, and he realised that in his innermost soul he had never wanted it.
>
> Yet he wanted *some* living fellowship with other men; as it was he was just isolated. Maybe a living fellowship!—but not affection, not love, not comradeship. Not mates and equality and mingling. Not blood-brotherhood. None of that.
>
> What else? He didn't know. . . . Perhaps the thing that the dark races know: that one can still feel in India: the mystery of lordship. . . . The mystery of innate, natural, sacred priority. The other mystic relationship between men, which democracy and equality try to deny and obliterate. Not any arbitrary caste or birth aristocracy. But the mystic recognition of difference and innate priority, the joy of obedience and the sacred responsibility of authority. (Pp. 120–21.)

In *The Plumed Serpent* this "mystic relationship" among men becomes one of the basic principles of a newly-founded religious state.

Lawrence tries to project an organic society across the pages of that novel, a society based on living contact between man and man, and between man and God as well. The basic faults of that society can be left for the final chapter; at present, we are chiefly concerned with personal relationships, and in this respect the leader-follower idea has a certain limited validity. There is a natural tendency towards dominance and submission, that is, in any human relationship: marriages and friendships are not miniature democracies, they are living and life-giving units which require direction as well as give and take. Lawrence did make a mistake, however, in siphoning off friendship and lordship into separate compartments, for without the leaven of common sympathy, "lordship" soon degenerates into sheer brutality;[6] but he was caught up in the larger problem of man's work with and among men, at the time, and even then he was quick to recognize the limitations of his position. With *The Plumed Serpent* behind him, he could write to Witter Bynner in 1928:

> On the whole, I think you're right. The hero is obsolete, and the leader of men is a back number. After all, at the back of the hero is the militant ideal: and the militant ideal, or the ideal militant seems to me also a cold egg. . . . On the whole I agree with you, the leader-cum-follower relationship is a bore. And the new relationship will be some sort of tenderness, sensitive, between men and men and men and women, and not the one up one down, lead on I follow, *ich dien* sort of business. So you see I'm becoming a lamb at last. . . . (*Letters* [Huxley], p. 711)

The tenderness theme, set forth that same year in *Lady Chatterley's Lover*, represents the third and final phase of the friendship problem.

---

[6] We see a good example of this in one of the early stories, "The Prussian Officer," as Captain Hauptmann persecutes his orderly, Schöner, to the point where Schöner murders him. Interestingly enough, Frank Amon, among others, has tried to read "psychological undertones of homosexuality" into this story (see *The Achievement of D. H. Lawrence*, ed. Hoffman and Moore, pp. 227-28). But Hauptmann is merely a fixed, rigid, inorganic creature, and what he resents in the orderly is his organic wholeness. As Lawrence tells us:

> He could not get away from the sense of the youth's person, while he was in attendance. It was like a warm flame upon the older man's tense, rigid body, that had become almost unliving, fixed. There was something so free and self-contained about him, and something in the young fellow's movement, that made the officer aware of him. And this irritated the Prussian. He did not choose to be touched into life by his servant. . . . To see the soldier's young, brown, shapely peasant's hand grasp the loaf or the wine-bottle sent a flash of hate or of anger through the elder man's blood. It was not that the youth was clumsy: it was rather the blind, instinctive sureness of movement of an unhampered young animal that irritated the officer to such a degree. (*The Portable D. H. Lawrence*, pp. 38-39.)

In other words, there is nothing homosexual about this relationship; it is simply the obverse of *Blutbrüderschaft*.

The lordship theme has been cast aside, and the brotherhood theme long since abandoned—though to be more accurate, both themes have been sharply modified, dropped to the background, and realigned within the larger scheme of the novel at hand. Now man and woman move forth refreshed from the central marriage unit, and bring the sense of touch or tenderness, which marriage has roused in them, to all their human relationships. Now Connie tells Mellors that the future depends on this gift of tenderness, and the gamekeeper replies by citing his experience as a leader of men in the first World War:

> Ay . . . You're right. It's that really. It's that all the way through. I knew it with the men. I had to be in touch with them, physically, and not go back on it. I had to be bodily aware of them and a bit tender to them, even if I put 'em through hell. It's a question of awareness, as Buddha said. But even he fought shy of the bodily awareness, and that natural physical tenderness, which is the best, even between men, in a proper manly way. Makes 'em really manly, not so monkeyish. (P. 335.)

"That natural physical tenderness . . . even between men, in a proper manly way." Lawrence corrects here his overemphasis on physical, nonsexual male communion in *Women in Love;* he arrives, further, at a valid mode of approach to life, at a change in being and a change, even, in the quality of human relationships; but he does not wholly solve the problem posed in *Women in Love,* because, it seems, that problem is insoluble. There must always be a certain amount of conflict between a man's friendships, however deep, and his love for his wife, since marriage is always *central* to his fulfillment, while friendships are peripheral and expendable, though paradoxically vital.[7] Yet Lawrence brings us, nonetheless, a vivid sense of this everpresent conflict: by plunging into basic human complications, by emerging, eventually, in some new direction, with new problems posed and old ones solved, exhausted, or laid aside unsolved, he broadens and deepens the scope of our own strait-jacket lives, and makes us face the full extent of our own dilemmas. For as William Blake would have it, we never know what is enough unless we know what is more than enough.

---

[7] As Lawrence puts it in a late essay:

> A woman is one bank of the river of my life, and the world is the other. Without the two shores, my life would be a marsh. It is the relationship to woman, and to my fellow-men, which makes me myself a river of life. . . .
>
> But the relationship of man to woman is the central fact in actual human life. Next comes the relationship of man to man. And, a long way after, all the other relationships, fatherhood, motherhood, sister, brother, friend. (*Phoenix,* pp. 192–93.)

The Substance of *Women in Love*

by Eliseo Vivas

I

While the two main themes, the development of which defines the organization of *Women in Love,* are the love affair of Birkin and Ursula and the liaison of Gerald and Gudrun, the substance of the novel cannot be adequately defined in terms of the love affairs alone. The novel is a very ambitious book whose substance consists of the elucidation of the theme of human destiny at a given moment in history in terms of the conditions in which the four main characters find themselves. If I am right, and I hope to validate my judgment in this chapter, Lawrence could have claimed much more than he did when, defending himself from a criticism, he wrote to Edward Garnett in a phrase already cited that he was "a passionately religious man," and that his novels had to be written from the depths of his religious experience.[1] In *Women in Love* religion, as ordinarily understood, does not enter: man's relation to God is not part of the substance of the novel; but Lawrence poses the problem of human destiny in view of the fact that his characters cannot believe in God, so that religion, by its failure, defines the central problem of the novel.

It is only when we put *Women in Love* in this perspective that we are able to see clearly the relation of Lawrence to the most profound and most challenging movement in contemporary philosophy in our Western world, atheistic existentialism. Nietzsche's exultant cry, "God is dead!" is one of Sartre's starting points. God's death forces the atheistic philosopher to face the problem of destiny in ultimate, radical, and desperate terms. And it was in these terms that Lawrence faced the same problem. The philosophy of love, the religion of the blood, the

---

"The Substance of Women in Love" by Eliseo Vivas. From D. H. Lawrence: The Failure and Triumph of Art (Evanston, Ill.: Northwestern University Press, 1960), pp. 237–54, in abridged form. Copyright © 1960 by Northwestern University Press. Reprinted by permission of Northwestern University Press and George Allen and Unwin Ltd. (For a more theoretical discussion of the "constitutive symbol" see Vivas' chapter so titled. Also see Robert B. Heilman, p. 97–103, below.)

[1] *Letters,* p. 193.

"leader-*cum*-follower" program—all his ideas, solutions, insights, and messages, significant as they are by themselves, achieve full significance only when we see them as attempts to discover a way of life that would center, "seeing there is no God." And it is only when we put Lawrence in this perspective that we are able to see fully what kind of novelist he was. Most contemporary novelists are moralists—or immoralists as the case may be. Witness Conrad and Gide. I do not mean that they preach or have a message; I mean that the matter they seek to elucidate by transforming it into the substance of art is the stuff of human relations. Only very few are, if I may so call them, "cosmologists," in the sense that their matter is man's relation to the cosmos. This was the matter Dreiser sought to transform into the substance of art, as I have indicated elsewhere. And this is the "problem" that, in the last analysis, obsessed Lawrence. That he "failed," in the sense that not one of his "answers" was acceptable and viable, is a relatively minor consideration. He posed the problem; and this, in philosophy and in poetry, is all, or nearly all that we can expect. An honest man today, whether for him God is dead or living, knows, knows in his entrails, as Unamuno would have put it, that there is no easy answer to his cosmic query, no easy way out of his radical predicament.

And finally, from the critical standpoint, it is only when we make explicit Lawrence's basic theme or problem that we are able to appreciate in their full value the role played by some of the components in defining and elucidating that problem. Why are Hermione's values false? Why must Gerald die? What is the importance of the discussion of the African figurine in Halliday's flat? The answer is that neither Hermione's cerebral values nor Gerald's ethics of productivity can serve as a substitute for God. But the African way may serve, although Lawrence would have us believe that Birkin finally rejects it. It is in a sort of "ultimate marriage" that Birkin finds an adequate substitute for God. This, at any rate, is what Lawrence would have us believe. What the novel says is not the same thing. But while the novelist remains what we have already seen him to be, a dribbling liar, the novel does not suffer from his lies: for the truth of the novel is not in disruptive conflict with the lies of the novelist; it is to be found below them.

II

The repudiation of the ethics of productivity and of the machine, as embodied in the colliery, is not new in Lawrence's work. We found it in *The Rainbow*, conveyed powerfully by Ursula's reaction to her uncle and the colliery he manages. (In mentioning Ursula here, I am not suggesting that the two novels are continuous; I do not think they are, although we know they were carved from a single novel entitled *The Sisters*.) In *Women in Love* Lawrence offers us a more detailed account of the essential weakness of the man who serves the machine and the flaws of the ethics of productivity than he offered us in *The Rainbow*. Carefully he draws a contrast between Gerald and the older Crich, and between Gerald and Rupert. The father manages the mines paternalistically and inefficiently while Gerald is pure efficiency and "go." And Gerald's love life is shallow while Rupert's is deep in spite of the conflicts that thwart him. This contrast is brought out by dialogue, by actual description, and by means of a number of semiotic signs and constitutive symbols, all of which converge to give us a picture of Gerald. The power of the Industrial Magnate is a sham. He is killed by the woman and the German whom Gerald thinks of as a "little vermin."

As I have already mentioned in a different connection, in Chapter IV, "Diver," Gudrun sees Gerald dive and swim and envies him for his "freedom, liberty and mobility," and Ursula tells Gudrun about his improvements of Shortlands, his "go," and the way in which the miners hate him. In Chapter V, "In the Train," through the conversation between Birkin and Gerald, we are given a fairly clear account of Gerald's callousness, glistening through "the ethics of productivity." And we are also informed that he is satisfied to let his life be artificially held together by the social mechanism. In the semiotic sign or quasi-symbol of the mare scene, in Chapter IX, "Coal-Dust," we are given a picture of Gerald's ruthlessness. The Brangwen sisters are on the way home from school and the colliery train is rumbling near. They know Gerald only slightly at this time. Lawrence tells us:

> Whilst the two girls waited, Gerald Crich trotted up on a red Arab mare. He rode well and softly, pleased with the delicate quivering of the creature between his knees. . . . The locomotive chuffed slowly between the banks, hidden. The mare did not like it. She began to wince away, as if hurt by the unknown noise. But Gerald pulled her back and held her head to the gate.—CHAPTER IX

I need not quote any more. The mare tries to bolt but Gerald forces her back. "The fool!" cried Ursula loudly. "Why doesn't he ride away till it's gone by?" The struggle goes on. "And she's bleeding! She's bleeding!" cries Ursula, while Gudrun looks and the world reels and passes into nothingness for her.

We have already seen that throughout his career Lawrence brooded long and deeply, almost obsessively, on the Gerald type and that he contrasted it with the type of the gamekeeper. In *The Rainbow* Gerald had a small part to play in the form of Tom Brangwen, Ursula's uncle. Sometimes he is metamorphosed into an emasculated Clifford Chatterley, and sometimes into an intellectual or a member of an artistic group such as the Bricknells and their friends in *Aaron's Rod*. He also appears, as we saw, as the effete rich young man, Rico. There is an important difference between Gerald and his imitations: the presentation of Gerald's deficiencies and limitations is achieved in dramatic terms. Whatever the sources of his conception (and the combination of Major Barber and Middleton Murry could not, on the surface, have appeared more incongruous and less promising than they evidently were) the result is a person grasped directly, not in terms of concepts, a moving, responding, human being, whose industrial success, whose inward disorganization and failure in love are not the product of a philosophy on the part of their creator, but a genuinely creative conception. Gerald is an industrialist moved by a strong will to power, a man whose world does not center. Having succeeded as a mine owner, he gets trapped in a love affair that kills him. And we are made to see, in terms of the relationship between him and Gudrun, why he had to die and how he was spiritually dead before he died physically.

Birkin, with whom Gerald is contrasted, is no less protean. He is the gamekeeper in *Lady Chatterley,* sometimes he is a gypsy, a southern Italian, a Mexican general of pure Indian blood, a Bohemian count, a groom, and once even a horse. The contrast in its many allotropic manifestations is the expression of a kind of Manichean conception of life in which the gamekeeper type is the fountain of life, potency, and tenderness; the Gerald type, often sexually impotent, is the bearer of corruption, causing destruction of self and of others. One could say, it is Eros against Thanatos.

It is important to notice the difference between the two types. The gamekeeper is always conceived in authentic dramatic terms; he is created out of pure experience. But this is not the case with the Gerald type. In *The Rainbow* Tom Brangwen, Ursula's uncle, although not a fully developed personality, is as authentic as any one in the book. And, with a qualification to be made next, this holds for Gerald. However, the Gerald type soon becomes a dramatized concept, an idea dressed up as a man, and sometimes—as in the case of the clergyman, Mr. Massy, in "The Daughters of the Vicar"—a mere caricature whose function in the story is to serve as a foil and a cathartic stimulus for Lawrence's hatred.

The qualification that must be entered is that the business magnate aspect of Gerald is not conceived in an utterly dramatic manner. There is in him something of the dramatized idea, and that is the reason we can apprehend this aspect of Gerald in terms of semiotic symbols without remainder. The mare scene is not at all a constitutive symbol and its meaning is given us discursively in Chapter XII, "Carpeting," and in XVII, "The Industrial Magnate." In the first of these two chapters the

Brangwen sisters criticize Gerald for his cruelty to the mare, and Gerald defends himself on the ground that the mare must be taught to stand if it is to be of use to him. And in the second of these chapters, which contains a fairly complete account of the contrasting philosophies of industry held by the older owner, Thomas Crich, and his son, Gerald, the picture of both men is given discursively and conceptually. All the chapter does, therefore, is to fill out the details of what we already know about Gerald, and what we know about him is something Lawrence states fully by means of a combination of behavioral traits and a statement of Gerald's ideology. When he takes over the management of the mines from his father, Gerald abandons the benevolent paternalism with which the mines have been managed. He has conceived the idea of "the pure instrumentality of mankind," and what he wants is "the pure fulfillment of his own will in the struggle with the natural conditions. His will was now to take the coal out of the earth profitability." What "mattered was the great social productive machine." Gerald now had his life work, which was "to extend over the earth a great perfect system in which the will of man ran smoothly and unthwarted, timeless, a Godhead in process." I hope it can be noticed from the snippets I have quoted that the picture of Gerald, however behavioral, is essentially a conceptual one. We understand Gerald as we understand the Robber Barons or as we understand Don Juan. Don Juan may be different from Casanova, and Don Juan Tenorio may be different from Don Giovanni, but the difference lies on the surface and we conceive of them in essentially the same terms and these terms are more conceptual than dramatic.

An essential part of Lawrence's concept of Gerald the industrial magnate is the emptiness of the man, and this is also stated conceptually, although the discursive statement does not do justice to the dramatic presentation we also find in *Women in Love*. We are told that once Gerald succeeds in overhauling the system and in making the mines pay, he is up against the horror of his own vacuity:

> But now he had succeeded—he had finally succeeded. And once or twice lately, when he was alone in the evening and had nothing to do, he had suddenly stood up in terror, not knowing what he was. And he went to the mirror and looked long and closely at his own face, at his own eyes, seeking for something. He was afraid, in mortal dry fear, but he knew not what of. . . . He was afraid that one day he would break down and be a purely meaningless bubble lapping round a darkness.
>
> But his will yet held good, he was able to go away and read, and think about things.—CHAPTER XVII

His will holds good, after a fashion, until Gudrun and Loerke make a concerted and successful, if unconscious, effort to kill him.

But Gerald is more than a business magnate; he is also a friend and a lover, and these other sides of his personality are not dramatized illustrations of concepts. . . .

*   *   *

. . . and cannot be "reduced" to abstract terms. . . . Take for instance, the scene in which the rabbit, Bismarck, unites Gerald and Gudrun in a demonic marriage, Chapter XVIII. It will be remembered that Gerald and Gudrun never actually "marry" in a conventional sense and they do not begin living together until later. But it is in the rabbit scene that their ritual union finally takes place. To be present at an obscenity is, of course, literally speaking, an impossibility, if we take the term in its primitive sense. But the very paradox of our witnessing that which is out of sight while we are spectators in front of the stage, emphasizes the fact intended objectively by the scene, namely that there is something beyond the ordinary, beyond the presentable in the mystic communion of Gerald and Gudrun of which the officiating priest is a kicking, angry rabbit, and the witness is a child. Bringing to a final ripening the relationship between Gerald and Gudrun, the symbolic episode of the rabbit recapitulates dramatically the understanding that they had reached earlier and throws light on the experience that is to follow.

At the time of the rabbit episode a considerable degree of understanding had already been arrived at between Gerald and Gudrun. The first time Gudrun saw Gerald at his sister's wedding (Chapter I), she had reacted strongly to his presence, wanting to be alone, to know the strange, sharp inoculation that had changed the whole temper of her blood. From there on we begin to realize gradually that the relationship is going to generate a destructive force the victim of which will be Gerald. But although the scenes in which the destructive action is presented are stages in the development of an understanding between the two and contribute to our grasp of the quality of their relationship, they do not fully give us that quality. And what is much more important, no adjective or combination of adjectives seems adequate to characterize the quality of the relationship. When it finally comes to its catastrophic ending, the inadequacy of such characterization is more obvious. To call the relationship antagonistic is completely inadequate, since until the very end there is a kind of love between the two of them. But it would be no less inadequate to call it ambivalent. In the final analysis it is ineffable in abstract terms, and nothing but the full synoptic grasp of the chapters in which it is dramatically defined will yield its complexity, its nuances, the ebb and flow of its passion, and its corrosive destructiveness. Gerald and Gudrun move towards one another to their fulfillment, and the union is disastrous for Gerald, although they do not engage in the frightfully intense fights that Birkin and Ursula engage in. Gudrun's early slapping of Gerald's face is not an attack welling out of mutual irritation and lack of understanding. And the final fight in which Gerald almost chokes Gudrun to death is not occasioned—although it is easy to misunderstand it—by Gerald's jealousy of Loerke. How then are we to grasp the essentially negative nature of their relationship? As we turn the matter in our minds we become convinced to our dismay that discursive language can do no justice to it. Whatever there is between the man and the woman wells up from the depths of their souls; nor is it something to be *understood,* if the term is used to stand for the exhibition of motivations that can be more or less accurately designated in psychological language. But when we turn to the episode of the rabbit and consider the experience between Gerald and Gudrun in the light this episode throws upon it, the whole relationship becomes an object of dramatic aesthesis. What precedes the rabbit episode is crystallized and can now be grasped fully as an object of immediate apprehension, and what follows it takes its significance from it. The rabbit scene is a constitutive symbol. The critic, in the last analysis, is impotent before such a symbol; all he can do is suggest some of the obvious discursive meanings that the scene evokes.

Gudrun and Winifred, Gerald's little sister, want to catch Bismarck in order to draw him, because he looks splendid and fierce. As they are on their way to the hutch Gerald appears, and in the middle of the conversation between him and Gudrun we are told that their eyes meet in knowledge and Gerald finds himself desiring Gudrun. Gerald goes away and Gudrun tries to catch the rabbit, although Winifred warns her that he is a fearful kicker. Gudrun seizes the rabbit by the ears, but he is very strong and in an instant he is lunging wildly and kicking in mid-air. Gudrun is having a hard time holding him when Gerald returns and takes the rabbit from her. The beast lashes out at him also and Gerald, swift as lightning, brings his hand down on his neck. The rabbit emits an unearthly, abhorrent scream and is finally subdued. But nothing but the actual passage will do, although in order for it to have its full effect it must be read in context:

> "You wouldn't think there was all that force in a rabbit," he [Gerald] said, looking at Gudrun. And he saw her eyes black as night in her pallid face, she looked almost unearthly. The scream of the rabbit, after the violent tussle, seemed to have torn the veil of her consciousness. He looked at her, and the whitish, electric gleam in his face intensified.
>
> "I don't really like him," Winifred was crooning. "I don't care for him, as I do for Loozie. He's hateful really."
>
> A smile twisted Gudrun's face, as she recovered. She knew she was revealed.
>
> "Don't they make the most fearful noise when they scream"? she cried, the high note in her voice, like a seagull's cry.

"Abominable," he said.

"He shouldn't be so silly when he has to be taken out," Winifred was saying, putting out her hand and touching the rabbit tentatively, as it skulked under his arm, motionless as if it were dead.

"He's not dead, is he, Gerald?" she asked.

"No, he ought to be," he said.

"Yes, he ought!" cried the child, with a sudden flush of amusement. And she touched the rabbit with more confidence. "His heart is beating *so* fast. Isn't he funny? He really is."

"Where do you want him?" asked Gerald.

"In the little green court," she said.

Gudrun looked at Gerald with strange, darkened eyes, strained with underworld knowledge, almost supplicating, like those of a creature which is at his mercy, yet which is his ultimate victor. He did not know what to say to her. He felt the mutual hellish recognition. And he felt he ought to say something, to cover it. He had the power of lightning in his nerves, she seemed like a soft recipient of his magical, hideous white fire. He was unconfident, he had qualms of fear.

"Did he hurt you?" he asked.

"No," she said.

"He's an insensible beast," he said, turning his face away.

They came to the little court. . . . Gerald tossed the rabbit down. It crouched still and would not move. Gudrun watched it with faint horror.

"Why doesn't it move?" she cried.

"It's skulking," he said.

She looked up at him, and a slight sinister smile contracted her white face.

"Isn't it a *fool!*" she cried. "Isn't it a sickening *fool?*" The vindictive mockery in her voice made his brain quiver. Glancing up at him, into his eyes, she revealed again the mocking, white-cruel recognition. There was a league between them, abhorrent to them both. They were implicated with each other in abhorrent mysteries.

"How many scratches have you?" he asked, showing his hard forearm, white and hard and torn in red gashes.

"How really vile!" she cried, flushing with a sinister vision. "Mine is nothing."

She lifted her arm and showed a deep red score down the silken white flesh.

"What a devil!" he exclaimed. But it was as if he had had knowledge of her in the long red rent of her forearm, so silken, and soft. He did not want to touch her. He would have to make himself touch her, deliberately. The long, shallow red rip seemed torn across his own brain, tearing the surface of his ultimate consciousness, letting through the forever unconscious, unthinkable red ether of the beyond, the obscene beyond.

"It doesn't hurt you very much, does it?" he asked solicitous.

"Not at all," she cried.

And suddenly the rabbit, which had been crouching as if it were a flower, so still and soft, suddenly burst into life. Round and round the

The Substance of Women in Love 93

court it went, as if shot from a gun, round and round like a furry meteorite, in a tense hard circle that seemed to bind their brains. They all stood in amazement, smiling uncannily, as if the rabbit were obeying some unknown incantation. Round and round it flew, on the grass under the old red walls like a storm.

And then quite suddenly it settled down, hobbled among the grass, and sat considering, its nose twitching like a bit of fluff in the wind. After having considered for a few minutes, a soft bunch with a black, open eye, which perhaps was looking at them, perhaps was not, it hobbled calmly forward and began to nibble the grass with that mean motion of a rabbit's quick eating.

"It's mad," said Gudrun. "It is most decidedly mad."

He laughed. "The question is," he said, "what is madness? I don't suppose it is rabbit-mad."

"Don't you think it is?" she asked.

"No. That's what it is to be a rabbit."

There was a queer, faint, obscene smile over his face. She looked at him and saw him, and knew that he was initiate as she was initiate. This thwarted her, and contravened her, for the moment.

"God be praised we aren't rabbits," she said, in a high, shrill voice.

The smile intensified a little, on his face.

"Not rabbits?" he said, looking at her fixedly.

Slowly her face relaxed into a smile of obscene recognition.

"Ah, Gerald," she said, in a strong, slow, almost man-like way. "—All that, and more." Her eyes looked up at him with shocking nonchalance.

He felt again as if she had hit him across the face—or rather, as if she had torn him across the breast, dully, finally. . . . —CHAPTER XVIII

There is a suggestion that the marriage ritual performed by the officiating rabbit is consummated by the blood drawn by the animal's clawing. But if this seems too ingenious, certainly the gash will be recognized by the reader as a variant of the face-slapping episode and an anticipatory summation of their subsequent relationship. One of the themes that the rabbit episode illumines is expressed several times through the novel and comes to indirect and periphrastic expression in Chapter XXI, entitled "Threshold." In the midst of a conversation between Gerald and Gudrun on Birkin's ideal of marriage, we read:

And they both [Gerald and Gudrun] felt the subterranean desire to let go, to fling away everything, and lapse into a sheer unrestraint, brutal and licentious. A strange black passion surged up pure in Gudrun. She felt strong. She felt her hands so strong, as if she could tear the world asunder with them. She remembered the abandonments of Roman licence, and her heart grew hot. She knew she wanted this herself also—or something, something equivalent. Ah, if that which was unknown and suppressed in her were once let loose, what an orgiastic and satisfying event it would be. And she wanted it, she trembled slightly from the proximity of the man, who stood just behind her, suggestive of the same black licentiousness that rose in herself. She wanted it with him, this unacknowledged frenzy. For a moment the clear perception of this preoccupied her, distinct and perfect in its final reality. . . . —CHAPTER XXI

From *Women in Love* it is not possible to discover exactly what their subterranean desire consisted of. But we have already seen what is intended in *Lady Chatterley's Lover*—practices encountered in Krafft-Ebing. Another suggestion of this sort is to be found in *The Rainbow*, in which, describing the love life of Will and Anna, Lawrence tells us that it had become

> a sensuality violent and extreme as death. They had no conscious intimacy, no tenderness of love. It was all the lust and the infinite, maddening intoxication of the senses, a passion of death.

And Lawrence continues:

> . . . Awful and threatening it was, dangerous to a degree, even whilst he gave himself to it. It was pure darkness, also. All the shameful things of the body revealed themselves to him now with a sort of sinister, tropical beauty. All the shameful, natural and unnatural acts of sensual voluptuousness which he and the woman partook of together, created together, they had their heavy beauty and their delight. Shame, what was it? It was part of extreme delight. It was that part of delight of which man is usually afraid. Why afraid? The secret, shameful things are most terribly beautiful.
>
> They accepted shame, and were one with it in their most unlicensed pleasures. It was incorporated. It was a bud that blossomed into beauty and heavy, fundamental gratification.—CHAPTER VIII

It is not possible to be dogmatic on this question, but I suggest that these passages throw light on a recurrent preoccupation of Lawrence's fictional characters which we have already encountered in *The Plumed Serpent*. We find the same preoccupation in the short story, "The Fox." This story is, almost to the end, a perfectly worked out dramatic situation containing, in the figure of the fox, a powerfully suggestive constitutive symbol. But all of a sudden, after the marriage of Henry and Nellie, the story takes a wholly unexpected and incongruous turn, because Nellie exerted herself in her love towards Henry and he would not have it:

> If she was in love, she ought to *exert* herself, in some way, loving. She felt the weary need of our day to *exert* herself in love. . . . No, he would not let her exert her love towards him. No, she had to be passive, to acquiesce, and to be submerged under the surface of love.[2]

This passage comes all of a sudden, without any relation to what preceded it, without preparation, and the reader is aware that the story has taken, for a reason he does not know, a new turn.

[2] *The Tales of D. H. Lawrence*, p. 476.

These quotations—and many more could be given—enable us to grasp the fact that the love relationship of some of Lawrence's fictional characters involves, besides their Krafft-Ebing aspect, or perhaps, because of it, an animal quality of hardness and cruelty. Their mating, we come to realize, is like the mating of those insects in which the female kills the male after or even during the act. This reinforces, in turn, our sense that, in *Women in Love,* the apparently strong industrial magnate turns out to be the weaker of the two and the woman knows it from the beginning. She finally sends Gerald to his death when she is done with him and finds her true mate in the German sculptor, Loerke. Gudrun murders Gerald without premeditation, guile, or plan, in a more or less unconscious manner, by forcing him to face the frozen emptiness of his soul. This is not at all clear during the black rite at which the rabbit officiates. Nor are the premonitions that have preceded the black rite of their marriage fully clear at this point. They become clear—in the sense in which an ordered presentation can be grasped as aesthetically clear—when we manage to comprehend synoptically the whole poem.

It seems desirable to expatiate upon a point already touched on in another connection but not fully elucidated. We have abundant evidence that Lawrence took the account of Gerald as a general law, which may be formulated as follows: industrial magnates are weak and therefore incapable of adequate fulfillment as human beings. But his acceptance of this law does not constitute a fault in *Women in Love,* and the question whether the law is true or false is not relevant, for *Women in Love* has been conceived initially in dramatic terms. What is relevant is that in the novel the way in which Gerald's life is held together externally by the ethics of productivity, the inward emptiness of his life, its tropism towards self-destruction, the eventual failure of his affair with Gudrun and his disastrous fate—all are accepted by the reader as making a harmonious whole. This was the way Gerald was and this was his fate, and there is nothing in his actions or words, nothing in the whole account of him that forces us to recognize the picture as factitious. But a fact and an explanation of a fact are two different things, and if one asks why the combination of traits and inclinations constituting Gerald lead him to his disastrous end, the answer that in fact they do is not an answer to the question. However, it is advisable to reiterate with emphasis that the only admissible question is whether or not dramatically there is a clash or confusion, a disharmony or incongruity, that prevents us from accepting the drama as presented. If there is none, the question, whatever its historical validity or importance, does not point to a flaw because in the novel we find no answer to it. The observation is important not merely because it points to the high achievement that *Women in Love* is generally conceded to represent, but because it calls attention by contrasts to the relative failure of those of Lawrence's works in which the component parts are held together mechanically, are tied together by dramatized conceptual means, are, in short, factitious. The contrast marks the difference between the high point of his creative power and lesser expressions of it. It is important to bear in mind that the lesser expressions are by no means negligible, if we are to appreciate the full miracle of his achievement.

That the question of adequate causation does not arise, however, deserves further attention, at least to this extent: Gerald is a successful creation. But when we take it all in and try to see what Lawrence has done and how he has done it, we are forced to reconsider our judgment. Highly as we may have thought of the novel before the critical exploration had done its job, we are now forced to go further and to admit that it is the product of an artistic talent that is quite rare. For it is not in the cattle and the rabbit scenes alone that we find constitutive symbols by means of which Lawrence accomplishes the feat of concentrating meanings and associations he wishes to reveal. The novel presents Gerald by means of a cluster of component constitutive symbols, although, if I am right, all the other symbols occupy a place subordinate to that of the rabbit. Indeed, if the word were not so misleading, because of its polysemic richness, I would say that *Women in Love* is a triumph of *symbolic* art: of art that works, in Mr. Leavis' phrase, from profounder levels and in more complex ways in order to convey more and deeper significance than naturalistic or realistic art is able to.

PART TWO

View Points

Robert B. Heilman

Vivas bases his criticism on A. C. Bradley's distinction between "matter for" and "informed substance of" art. In his discovery and perfecting of form by his imagination, the artist is not merely imitating and selecting but is creating (this is like the Coleridge view, as expounded by Richards). He is a "maker" and what he makes is a "poem." He fails creatively if he does not "transsubstance" the raw materials but leaves it untransformed autobiography or preachment, "bullying passion" or "autocratic ideology." When the raw material is transmuted, the substance is "dramatic" or "presented"; only then does it engage "intransitive attention." These principles are indispensable for anyone who acknowledges that the essence of art is the integration of form and substance.

As we have seen, Vivas devotes considerable time to discriminating between "untransformed matter" and "informed substance" in Lawrence. But he goes on to make his crowning point by distinguishing between the "superior quality" of *Sons and Lovers* and the greater achievement of *Rainbow* and *Women in Love*. The excellence of the latter two he attributes to Lawrence's extraordinary use of the "constitutive symbol," that is, "a symbol whose referent cannot be fully exhausted by explication, because that to which it refers is symbolized not only *through* it but *in* it." Here he is giving more precise theoretical form to Harry Moore's passing observation (in his 1950 volume) that Lawrence "used 'dynamic' symbols to convey inward states not ordinarily expressible in denotative language" and secured effects "of a *symboliste* kind," and to Leavis's notion of the "highly charged" scene. In Vivas's view the "meaning" is inherent in the creative symbol and cannot be apprehended independently of it; that is, it cannot be paraphrased, though fortunately Vivas does not wholly resist the temptation to try some prosaic restatements of such constitutive symbols as Gudrun's dancing before the bullocks. The scene which communicates in this absolute fashion might also be called the "expressionist symbol"—a

---

From "Nomad, Monads, and the Mystique of the Soma," by Robert B. Heilman (*a review of Eliseo Vivas'* D. H. Lawrence: The Failure and the Triumph of Art), in Sewanee Review, LXVIII (1960), 650–56. Copyright © 1960 by The University of the South. Reprinted by permission of the author and the publisher.

term which, in calling to mind Lawrence's affiliation with expressionism, would have the utility of suggesting an intensification and specialization of effect of which the standard price is a great attenuation of human range and fullness. Vivas's idea of the constitutive symbol is a helpful one; its disadvantage is that it gives primacy to the composition of the scene and gets away from the composition of the whole. But Lawrence's art drives an admirer toward such an emphasis.

Vivas makes a point of raising objections to Lawrence's ideas, characters, and scenes only when these remain as "matter" and have not undergone imaginative creation into "informed substance." If I understand him, one may approach the untransformed by asking questions that would not be suitable in dealing with informed substance. Failures abide our question; achieved art is free. Aaron is imperfectly "presented" by dramatic means; hence we may attack him with "Why?" and "What?" Except for some details we intuit Gerald Crich as aesthetically perfected; hence we may not ask why his combination of traits leads to disaster. We may not ask whether there is a valid general law that "industrial magnates are weak and therefore incapable of adequate fulfillment as human beings." We "need not" go into the question of whether emotional states felt in church by Lydia, Anna, and Will "can or cannot be properly called a religious experience." We may not question whether Birkin's presumptive fear of women "is or is not universal." We may not ask whether his doctrine of love is "by objective standards" an "expression of the good life." The essence of a novel is that it is a "dramatic presentation"; what it is a presentation of is irrelevant. "... we must take it or leave it. This is the way these people are—...."

Two motives appear here, and one must sympathize with both of them. One is strategic: to prevent a priori attitudes to "matter" from superseding the judgment of "informed substance," i.e., to keep politics out of art, or to revoke the critical franchise of those who simply class Lawrence as a great moralist or a voice of evil. The other is the technical rigorism of the aesthetician. But interestingly enough, Vivas has some nostalgia for the problems that the precisian in him feels compelled to dismiss; he even tends to shift ground. When, in discussing the obscene, he terms certain materials "unpleasant," he appears to glide from the aesthetic "The rendering is all" to the aesthetic "Not all things may be rendered," and the implication is that the thing rendered qualifies the rendering, or that the matter in some way asserts itself qualitatively in the informed substance. It is at least questionable whether one can wholly sever the issue of the representativeness of Crich's disintegration and of Birkin's gynophobia, or of the relevance to human potential of the Brangwen religious emotions and the Birkin erotology, from the issue of the aesthetic status of the forms in which these are rendered. When Vivas tells us that *Sons and Lovers* is not Lawrence "at his fullest and ripest" because it "does not embody the substance of his vision," he is invoking another criterion than that of successful rendering. When he says that the Birkin-Ursula affair is, in the original sense, *"idiotic,"* or that he does "not admire" "The Woman Who Rode Away" because "its substance, although wholly transmuted matter, is . . . wholly negative and masochistic," or mentions a hypothetical poet "greater, more universal, and more healthy than Lawrence," he reveals how much he is subject to a repressed conviction that the problem of art does involve more than the completeness and consistency of the "dramatic presentation." I would like to see Vivas trust to that conviction and engage in the formidable task of working out the structure of thought which it implies. For the doctrine that the measure of art is the adequacy of the transsubstancing process, though it has the advantage of defeating censorship and the sovietization of art, has the disadvantage of making all successful dramatic presentations equivalent (just as the doctrine of art as expression leaves one, as Brooks and Wimsatt point out, without grounds for making critical distinctions among different exercises in expression). Though we have a distaste for hierarchies of value, it seems imperative always to keep working at the resistant problem of the relative aesthetic status of dramatically realized works that transsubstance illness or health, the topical or the undated, the typical or the idiosyncratic, the part or the whole. The problem may be finally insoluble, and the attempting of it has manifest dangers; but not to attempt it may be more dangerous, for it may tacitly encourage the making of judgments and the claiming of authority by entirely noncritical centers of power. As far as Lawrence is concerned, the position that program is open to evaluation, but vision is not, leaves us without some fairly important instruments for the task of placing him.

The quest for logical purity in the aesthetic realm may cut a work off too sharply not only from its material cause but from the full reach of effects available to it. When Vivas insists that if we "feel sympathy for Ursula" in her reaction against a world of machines it is because our "minds were made up" beforehand, he seems to restrict aesthesis to a confirmatory role. Auden once argued that only second-rate art is corroborative ("That's just the way I always felt") and that true art alerts, awakens, forms, gives a sense of new illumination. Vivas is evidently intent on preserving "intransitive attention" against any possible infractions, and we may be sympathetic to this but at the same time propose that the contemplative act need not be static but may legitimately contain an openness to revelation. We need to distinguish between an incitement to nonaesthetic action which is a violation of intransitivity, and a modification of consciousness which is compatible with it.

Through such a modification of consciousness aesthesis may encompass what I have elsewhere called "feeling knowledge," which may be distinguished from a response to a rendering of the already known and felt.

Such a view of aesthesis is needed to make two important contentions of Vivas, one theoretical and one historical, tenable. If the artistic act is a creation, the apprehension of the created thing means the adaptation to a new sense of reality, with modifications that may extend even into the nonaesthetic realm of opinion; if we agree with the new creation, so to speak, only because we are already "with it," already have the insight implicit in it, then we have done the creating ourselves, and the artist is superfluous. If we are to accept the historical contention that Lawrence reveals our age to us, that he "charts our world," aids our "grasp of the modern world," we must acknowledge that intransitive attention naturally accommodates the acceptance of insights entirely new and perhaps positively disagreeable, and that this acceptance, far from springing from "our own implicit choices and commitments," may serve to reorder them. The point holds, of course, only if Lawrence reveals our world to us through a diagnosis which is implicit in his artistic transsubstancing of matter and through it becomes a force in our own imaginative constructions of reality. I am not sure of the mode of the Laurentian revelation. In some matters it appears that, instead of putting the finger on disorders, he simply embodies and exemplifies them: *Aaron's Rod,* Vivas says, "signifies . . . the widening area of infection which is poisoning our society." In Vivas's presentation, indeed, Lawrence is a confusing mixture of inspired prophet and exemplar of ruling vices, of the diagnostician and the pathological case—the diseased cell—that has diagnostic value for the study of the historic organism. If we can't always separate the two roles in him, we need to keep them apart theoretically: the man who shares in, reflects, and thus passively makes evident to others the nature of his times, hardly gets credit as artist or prophet. When it comes to illustrating lineaments, habits, and decay, tenth-rate writers do it just as well.

Vivas does not deal formally with Lawrence's style or theorize directly about the relation of style to successful creation. He mentions stylistic slumps now and then—the flatness of the writing in *Aaron's Rod,* the vagueness of that in *St. Mawr* (with a delightful note on how bad Lawrence is when he "of-it-alls us"). In the main he admires Lawrence for "his superb mastery over language." Of Lawrence's ability to actualize certain scenes—nature generally, flora and fauna, the appearance of people, erotic and other emotional states, and the instability of these—by original image, figure, and verbal arrangement there is no doubt. Along Willey Water "There was a rousedness and a glancing everywhere." "Something in him, inhuman and unmitigated, disturbed her." ". . . dangerous flamy sensitiveness." "Her face . . . full of baffled light." ". . . the night smashed." Along with such freshness there is a great deal of mawkishness: sentimental diminutives and so on. In general, there are two serious problems in Lawrence's style: one, repetitiousness, has often been noted; the other, though it is hinted at by Read and Dahlberg, is less recognized. I refer to a recurrent effeminacy; the stylistic aspect of a persistent incoherence in Lawrence is that often one page seems to have been written by a man, the next by a woman. This appears not only in style but in aspects of method; a female point of view is used more often than a male, and quite distractingly when the mystique of the soma informs the occasion. After *Sons and Lovers,* in which Paul actually notices Clara's breasts several times, and a scene or two in *Rainbow,* women hardly become physiologically real at all; but with disconcerting frequency the reader is put in the position of a woman gazing erotically at a man and tingling to his navel-to-knees equipment. The candid camera shots of men's life-giving loins, powerful buttocks, and thrilling thighs (always in tight pants in *The Plumed Serpent*) induce a "What goes on here?" state of mind that somewhat interferes with intransitive attention. The endeavor to define the transcendental revealed in coitus or other physical engagements often suggests the language of the seance or the "religious" advertisement which says, "Is your vital power attuned to the beyond?" Of a piece with his addiction to the female perspective is his persistent dropping into an effeminate vocabulary: the pervasive use of "so" as an intensive ("so glad," "so nervous"), of such adjectives as "pure," "real," "strange," and especially "horrible"; of "mystery" and "ecstasy," "trance" and "lapse" and "swoon." The Laurentian concordance of swoonerisms reflects a persistent collapsibleness, a softness of texture, an excess of fold and give. I am not sure that it is balanced by the constant echo of "potent male," "cruel," "hate," and "murder." Such "strong words" denote other moods: lunges out of swoons toward power, bursts into violence, often closer to tantrums than vigor. There is the quick impulse, the plunge, not steady strength and ordered movement.

To avoid overstatement, I must interpose the reminder that in Lawrence there is a large body of live, creative language that does not fall into such categories. But there is the problem of the obsessive repetition that Vivas, I believe, dismisses too quickly when he simply insists, without demonstration, on "what he achieves by means of it." Two kinds of repetition must be distinguished: the repeating of key words within a single passage, and the repeating of a couple of hundred basic words throughout a book and in book after book. The former seems to me almost uniformly successful; it provides a rhythmic emphasis that helps complete the scene. When it comes to the wholesale repetitions, we could distinguish several vocabularies that blossom widely: that of rather ordinary adjectives that can lead to flatness and slackness ("wild," "bright," "quick," etc., as Dahlberg points out); the Biblical images, allusions, paraphrases, and rhythms; the Lawrence trademark wordhoard. The ubiquitous Biblical should repay study: by it Lawrence often appears to be drawing on a traditional dignity and resonance to enhance events and feelings that lie outside of or even are counter to the tradition. The Lawrence specialties begin by catching the eye, challenging, puzzling, promising secrets; familiarity transforms them into idiom, an accepted argot divested of mystery; idiom sinks into cliché, but cliché that calls attention to itself, that is, mannerism. The prevalence of hyperbole in this private fashion prompts one involuntarily to frame a glossary: "annihilated" means "diminished," "dead" means "mortified," and so on. It will almost do, but not quite; though one can't help doing a lot of such scaling down as he goes along, the original is a little more than a trope of emphasis. But one nibbles at the problem of mannerisms and morals (which, for what it is worth, appears only slightly in *Sons and Lovers,* but keeps growing thereafter). What can one make of a world in which such substantives as these do the big business, ceaselessly hurtling at one like hard-sell entrepreneurs: blood, will, power, violence, malevolence, contact, potency, maleness, trance, nullity? When almost every state or condition that becomes dramatically significant is presented in tireless adjectives such as these: pure, naked, essential, electric, black, sensual, mental, proud, insolent, terrible, erect and prone, male and passive, potent, convulsive, wilful, corrupt, cruel, insidious, sinister? But above all, dark, mad, and mindless (the infinitely tedious mindless, which occurs scores of times to dozens of the others)? When the past participle is the queen verbal form, so that the focus is on the character to whom something is happening or being done: if he is doing well—fulfilled, completed, perfected, half-created or created, translated, transfigured, transported; if he is less well off—inchoate, suspended, unfulfilled, uncreated, convulsed, dazed, stunned, crushed, stupefied, nullified, destroyed, obliterated, disintegrated? Significantly, transitive verbs in active voice rarely become clichés: "hate" and "have power over" are among the few. In this world, the spontaneous and the masculine that are the proclaimed values are oddly infected with the feminine, the automatic, the passive, the categorical, the spasmodic and involuntary, with a queer mixture of the mechanical and the excessive, with the nonhuman. However one may characterize its moral quality, the mannerisms reveal an obsessive attachment to this world as presented—an unwillingness or inability to enlarge, complicate, enrich, or criticize it.

Such steps would lead to a constantly extending freedom of vocabulary.

Edwin Honig

Apparently the esthetic question concerning pastoral is subsumed under social and ethical matters which invariably attend upon the literary type. Pastoral dictates an idealized behavior that is protected from disillusioning consequences in the everyday world, while insisting upon its own standards as feasible, because imaginable and practicable, in the same world. Its tone and bias defy the fragmentations of everyday experience, and yet its examples—that is, specific events and the realistic behavior of people among the different classes—are covertly drawn from the world of contemporary actuality. Pastoral tries to show, as it were, how much brighter and hotter light may be when enclosed in a vacuum, and demands the same intensity of brightness and heat for the light existing outside the vacuum. It is a literature of recipe, which in part explains its attractiveness. It appeals to everyone who recognizes from his own experience the ingredients of which the recipe is composed—the discerning attitude of precocious children and misfit idealists, the wisdom of the poor and homely, the joys of the simple life, and the spontaneous expression of the passions between lovers. In this way it takes on a distinct social value. We all yearn for what we can imagine, even though it is unattainable. But how much more can we be made to want what is presented as possibly attainable after all!

Pastoral subsists in the practicability of its ideals and in its pointed criticism of all social behavior that falsifies or inhibits these ideals. In later examples of pastoral, the typical mock-heroics resound with deeper seriousness. The quixotism of Barnaby Rudge or Prince Mishkin raises the judicial principle above the shambles of hypocritical creeds. Also, in *Huckleberry Finn* or in the pastoral novels of Lawrence, Forster, and Conrad we find something more vital than the old back-to-nature formula or the blithe inducement to consort with shepherds or savages; we discover a criticism of civilized society's inability to produce an integrated individual, let alone a universal hero.

The critical attitude is made explicit in the typical Lawrence, Forster, or Conrad novel; there the hero is put into a situation which shows an idyllic surpassing of real-life adversity within credible nat-

---

From Dark Conceit: The Making of Allegory *by Edwin Honig (New York: Oxford University Press, 1966), pp. 165–68. Copyright © 1959 by Edwin Honig. Reprinted by permission of the author.*

uralistic surroundings. The hero's uncompromising nature challenges the heavy-footed class determinism or the sentimental amorality shackling the other characters. His superiority is especially evident when the hero's companion lacks his idyllic qualities and he is thus raised to the condition of being "vitally alone." The hero (or heroine) then serves mainly to urge other characters into a stricter awareness of themselves or to enact for them broader possibilities of self-realization. The hero becomes a case in point by overcoming the holocaust of a narrow determinism to which other characters succumb. D. H. Lawrence's *White Peacock* and *Women in Love* illustrate some of these general observations.

The pastoral elements in *The White Peacock* involve an unhappy crossing of classes and lovers against a landscape of perennial natural beauty. Always lowering, like the threat of a bad winter, is the society outside—the striking miners, the poachers, the evil squire, and his gamekeeper. The gamekeeper is a consistently fatalistic creature, who dies according to his own shallow determinism. On another level there is the romantic fatalism of George Saxton, who drinks himself to death. One is made to feel more particularly that George fails because he did not recognize a conviction of his own nature, which was to act when Lettie, his beloved, was ready to have him. In violating his own nature he violates the natural order. Thereafter, and as if in consequence, Lettie lapses into an unloving hollow sort of motherhood because she has accepted Leslie, the squire, instead of George. The gamekeeper is the unfulfilled noble savage, and George, the natural but weak aristocrat; Leslie represents the hardened remnant of an aristocracy that has lost its benevolent hold on society, and Lettie is the bluestocking whose "education" misguides her instincts. Because of sexual restraints, preconceived obligations to class, and betrayal of their basic nature, the inability of the characters to get along together becomes the reverberant moral note in the novel. And yet, though this approach to their relationships is nothing if not serious, one senses in it the constant encroachment of ludicrous forces that threaten to turn the novel into a sentimental melodrama.

In *Women in Love,* which concerns the problems of sexuality in love and friendship, Lawrence treats the pastoral elements more complexly. The first half of the novel wanders uncertainly as motives are planted among the characters. But beginning with the second half, minor characters and naturalistic preoccupations are discarded. Lawrence fastens on the relationship between two couples (Ursula and Birkin; Gudrun and Crich), and moves the narrative out of the tediously elaborated theme of isolation into a quickened sense of struggle and doom, where the strength of personal identity is constantly attacked by the passions. Basic to this interest is the impasse the sisters,

Ursula and Gudrun, create for their lovers, who consequently are forced into a close but ambiguous comradeship. There is no conventional hero among them; they are four violent forces of psychic appetite. Birkin wants love, but more than love a contact without commitment; he wants the possibility of love with one desirable woman and one desirable man. This he fails to achieve. He stands opposed, therefore, to Crich's negative animality just as Ursula, in her desire for full possession, stands opposed to Gudrun's passive narcissism. For Gudrun there is no limit except in her own helpless return to cruelty and sadism. For Ursula the limit is Birkin's sanction of her extreme need to consume and be consumed. Framing the four-sided sexual problem is the final pastoral landscape, fitting the predicament: the mountains of a Swiss ski resort in deathly frost and devastating whiteness. Here Crich dies, frozen at the bottom of a ravine. Subsequently Ursula comes to a curious mythic recognition of the ponderous animality that lies beneath Birkin's civilized self-delusion. Beside her as he drives the car, he grows stiff and monumental, "like an Egyptian Pharaoh," conveying both a real and an eternally unreal sense of animal potency. Here the reality would seem to be just as delusive as the unreality, since both depend upon something secret, insulated, and wishfully self-protective. This vitality which inexhaustibly feeds on itself is perhaps a terrible protraction of ingrown virginity. Ursula's realization, at any rate, deepens the desolate inconclusiveness of the main problem at the end.

Leone Vivante

Indeed spirit, identified with the creative essence, is everywhere where life is—i.e. spontaneous, nonmechanized, nonfactitious life. It is in sensation, in sensibility, in all sensuous material insofar as living, active quality. Sense merges harmoniously into the expression of the highest values, because these are already, *in principle,* in any sensuous reaction. Lawrence's very language seems to be quite consonant with this view, and to confirm it. He alludes, e.g., to "the profound sensual experience of truth." [1] He knows spirit in sense, which he sometimes calls the "flesh." Often it is only the "flesh" which shrinks from horrors planned by the abstract intellect and puts a limit to its excesses. We may ask, for what one-sidedness, blindness, and cruelty, is abstract

---

From A Philosophy of Potentiality *by* Leone Vivante *(London: Routledge & Kegan Paul Ltd., 1955), pp. 90–93, 102–4. Copyright © 1955 by Routledge & Kegan Paul Ltd. Reprinted by permission of the publisher.*

[1] *Last Poems,* 223 ("Satisfaction"). *Poems,* Heinemann, 720.

voluntary thought not responsible? The seed or kernel of harmonious truth, that "centrality" (again Lawrence's word) which we find in creative spontaneity, is found in sensibility rather than in the abstract intellect.[2]

It is Lawrence's conviction, I presume, that there cannot be any real knowledge of mental activity—of life, of the creative mystery—except through the experience of an immediate value and a sense of wonder. Compare, especially in this connection, the following passage from *The Rainbow:*

> "No, really," Dr. Frankstone had said, "I don't see why we should attribute some special mystery to life—do you? We don't understand it as we understand electricity, even, but that doesn't warrant our saying it is something special, something different in kind and distinct from everything else in the universe—do you think it does? May it not be that life consists in a complexity of physical and chemical activities, of the same order as the activities we already know in science? I don't see really, why we should imagine there is a special order of life, and life alone—"[3]

I see that Herbert Read, in his work *The Philosophy of Modern Art*,[4] points out even more explicitly the conflicting view which I here wish to emphasize. He quotes Dr. Johnson, who said: "We cease to wonder at what we understand"; and acutely adds: "It would have been much more to the point to have observed that understanding ceases when we cease to wonder."

Such expressions as "to know the unknown" or "the unknowable," or "the mystery," whenever they are found in Lawrence's writings, do not simply depend on the double meaning of the word "to know" (i.e. to know something *qua* object, externally and analytically—and to know through identification). They are meant to emphasize the knowledge, real knowledge, of something immense, which does not cease to be a mystery when it is known. Lawrence lays stress on the highly indeterminate and almost formless darkness—the relentless and yet tender power—the "life-quality" which is essentially mysterious in its very quality *qua* value.

A quite contrary attitude has asserted itself through the ages. According to it we would be inclined to conceive life, and the universe, as "absolved of mystery" (to use Lawrence's expression); and indeed almost as a plaything. We would simply admit, to explain life, a bit of chance—and automatic processes. First of all, we would overlook or deny all inward organic purposiveness in nature. The geneticist

---

[2] Cf. Letter to Ernest Collings, 17 Jan., 1913.
[3] *The Rainbow,* Heinemann, 1950 [1915], p. 440.
[4] New York, 1953, p. 141 (II, vi, *in fine*).

today traces the minutest individual characteristics to the genotype. Indeed, it seems to me, the power of the genotype suggests more than mechanism. But of course we should not properly speak of "power" in this connection, or in any connection whatever: rather of conditions which, through what is called natural and would better be called automatic selection, are bound to prevail.

Unhappily Lawrence himself says the opposite of what I have said above; or so it seems. He says that "knowledge and wonder counteract one another." [5] This is the generally accepted view. In a deterministically conceived world everything could be virtually foreseen (once we have accepted some ultimate datum), and insofar as it is foreseen it ceases to be marvellous or mysterious. But I imagine Lawrence was speaking here of what he calls "disintegrative knowledge." [6] "Disintegrative knowledge": a new and better expression for "abstractly objective" or "analytical" or "intellectualistic" knowledge—all unsatisfactory terms. This is the "ungodly knowledge," which "sunders," "divides," "cleaves," breaks "the kernel of truth," stifles, as it were, "the quick of life and truth," [7] and puts in its place a "life-substitute." [8] Indeed he uses often the words "knowledge" and "to know" in a quite derogatory sense. He says: "To know is to die." [9] In this sentence, I assume, "to know" means to know life or the psyche *as an object*. Cf. the passage: "Once the idea becomes explicit, it is dead. Yet we must *have* ideas." [10] To objectify is almost to take life away. Knowledge is apt to become an external construction on dead or half-dead presentments. It is no longer an identification with the "life-quality," which, in so far as it *is*, is only active, creative, a subject (active subject), not an object. In real knowledge, both in art and science, the separate self disappears: as Lawrence says, the will does not *interfere*.[11]

It is quite a different thing to know from the depth (cf. "he knows from the depth"),[12] or "to know in full," as he repeatedly says. What he condemns is ". . . the knowledge of the self-apart-from-God" [13]— apart from a reality which cannot be bereft of value and cannot be sundered from a sense of wonder.

The indeterminate—or infinite, or potential—really belongs to what

---

[5] *Assorted Articles*, "Hymns in Man's Life," Secker, London, 1913, p. 157.
[6] *Last Poems*, 26 ("The Hands of God").
[7] *Studies in Classic American Literature*, Secker, London, 1924, p. 83.
[8] *Fantasia of the Unconscious*, Heinemann, 1937 [1923], p. 128.
[9] *Id.*, 63.
[10] *Kangaroo*, Penguin Books, 1950 [1923], p. 291.
[11] *Fantasia of the Unconscious*, 67.
[12] *Poems*, 14.
[13] *Last Poems*, 144 ("God and the Holy Ghost").

Lawrence calls "upper consciousness." Yet, in his pursuit of the immense and almost formless, nocturnal power and in his rage against false reason and "automatic-logical" conclusions (his words, again),[14] Lawrence very frequently uses in a restricted and depreciative sense almost all the terms of the so-called "upper consciousness." This occurs especially in those writings which have a more explicit philosophical intent—where, as it seems to me, his thought is more assertive and his language more arbitrary. Yet we must not be misled: it remains true that his mental attitude is intensely and radically cognitive, contemplative-cognitive. He first of all vindicates the words of the spirit as against a merely practical and external or voluntaristic and antirationalistic point of view. The following passages confirm this:

> Conscience is being's consciousness, when the individual is conscious *in toto*, when he knows in full.[15]

> The Holy Ghost is the deepest part of our own consciousness
> wherein we know ourself for what we are
> and know our dependence on the creative beyond.[16]

The "unconscious" is not for him a word by which to explain away consciousness, or to supplant it. Consciousness remains for him the deepest and most general term for subjectivity. He conceives life and consciousness as inseparable.[17]

If he, not rarely, uses the word "thought," or "to think," disparagingly, this refers to the misplaced use of an externally constructive thought. He knows that, on any given occasion, the fault does not lie in thought, but in a defective, weak, cheap thought. For in a more reasoned and explicit thought the creative essence, the very source of harmonious truth, is easily—but not necessarily!—lost. In fact he says: "There are *few, few people* in whom the living impulse and reaction develops and sublimates into mental consciousness."[18]

* * *

What is the relation between individual consciousness and the feeling of the infinite as a self-transcendent living presence? Does not the latter submerge or annul the former? What is the relation between the individual and the collective consciousness? What is the relation

---
[14] *Fantasia of the Unconscious*, 67.
[15] *Id.*, 120.
[16] *Last Poems*, 144 ("God and the Holy Ghost").
[17] *Assorted Articles*, 23.
[18] *Fantasia of the Unconscious*, 74.

between the concept of a creative, living potentiality, or indeterminacy, and consciousness, freedom, and individuality?

Some quite distinct points must be stressed.

1. The creative essence—the creative being, to use Lawrence's expression,[19] the being which is in itself creative, the will-to-be, which as the words themselves seem to imply, is not entirely necessitated—once admitted, is quite intelligibly the perennial source of individuality. For one thing, it breaks the inert sequence of conditional causes, monotonously equated to one rigid necessity, the mechanical or eternal cause-and-effect relation, where there is no place for individuality. And even more intimately, it means newness, creative newness, and uniqueness; it makes individuality intelligible, rational.

2. The infinite urge—or, as Lawrence calls it, the "life-urge," "the Original, Creative Infinite" [20]—is an urge for form. It bears in its very core (as perhaps its primal motive-value, its ultimate *cause*) form, actualization—and individuality.

3. Potentiality, freedom, and consciousness are most closely related. A tied consciousness is no consciousness at all, its main-spring is cut.

4. The all-present infinite potency is felt as a value of universality, essentially dissatisfied with any limit whatever. Its purest spirit is especially antagonistic to the self-centered solidarity of a collective body, in which exclusiveness and pride prevail and all charity is exhausted within given, unpassable limits and becomes self-contradictory.

But these and other characteristics in the nature of mental reality do not help us to foresee and far less to influence the issue in the tremendous struggle between antagonizing values. From all we know in human history, and around us, the real enemy of individual consciousness, and individual responsibility, is not found in the materialistic conception—though, theoretically, this denies their ontological reality. Neither is it found in the direct relation between man and the incumbent creative mystery—its call for self-transcendency (which is heard in solitude, and still belongs to individualistic ethics). It is found in the organized collective will. The overpowerful collective consciousness, as in fact we know it, and as I think we ought to assume it must necessarily be, is a poor consciousness. There is no contemplation, no humility in it, no remorse, no doubting attitude, no intimate knowledge. It is exclusively practical, blindly practical. It is infatuated with emblems, symbols, liveries, rules, and customs, in which the collective will itself takes shape. It is fanatical, idolatrous;

---

[19] Cf. *St. Mawr*, 81.
[20] *Twilight in Italy*, 81.

above all cruel, capable of nameless atrocities. But it is extremely powerful. It has weapons which we must forgo, and it has many more points of vantage. Therefore the battle is unequal. However, not in vain, I hope, in the present great crossroads of history, Lawrence stands for freedom and consciousness, while he penetrates into the nature of consciousness and value and shows their nonpragmatical source.

The following passages may be quoted, as indicative of Lawrence's attitude in respect to this subject:

> There must be brotherly love, a wholeness of humanity. But there must also be pure, separate individuality, separate and proud as a lion or a hawk.[21]

> ... And I do think that man is related to the universe in some "religious" way, even prior to his relation to his fellow man.[22]

> While a man remains a man, before he falls and becomes a *social* individual, he innocently feels himself altogether within the great continuum of the universe.[23]

> ... So is every creature, even an ant or a louse, *individually* in contact with the great life-urge which we call God.[24]

> ... with a collective insect-like will, to avoid the responsibility of achieving any more perfected being or identity.[25]

There would be no end to the quotations. I shall only cite a few passages which regard quite another aspect of individuality: the meaning of physical, tangible, full materialization—the full value of *form* which we know only in the individual:

> ... the warm, white flame of a single life, revealing itself in contours that one might touch: a body! [26]

> The tangible unknown: that is the magic, the mystery, and the grandeur of love, that it puts the tangible unknown in our arms, and against our breast: the beloved. [27]

> ... (the) diabolic reducing down, disintegrating the vital organic body of life.[28]

---

[21] Quoted from *D. H. Lawrence Prophet of the Midlands*, by Vivian de Sola Pinto. Lecture given in the University of Nottingham, 1951, p. 17.
[22] *Stories, Essays, and Poems*, 409: Letter to Dr. Trigant Burrow, 3rd Aug., 1927.
[23] *Selected Essays*, 218 (*italics* mine).
[24] *Kangaroo*, 324 (*italics* mine).
[25] *The Plumed Serpent*, 114.
[26] *Lady Chatterley's Lover*, 86 (Chapter VI, p. three-but-one).
[27] *Kangaroo*, 150.
[28] *Women in Love*, [443].

Daniel A. Weiss

In his flight from his filial bondage Lawrence was trying to escape "the grey disease," as he called it, of mental consciousness. The imagery in which he envelops it, as for example in criticizing Marcel Proust, involves masturbation, which, like Swift's scatology, aroused his ultimate disgust. I equate Lawrence's rejection of mental consciousness with his rejection of his old incest fixation on his mother. The object of the original masturbation phantasy is, Freud insists, the mother herself. For Lawrence, in sexual relations an understanding between minds constituted a very real incest, implicit in the act of *knowing* someone sexually. To the psychologist, Dr. Trigant Burrow, Lawrence wrote:

> Do you know somebody who said: *on connait les femmes, ou on les aime; il n'y a pas de milieu?* It's Frenchy, but I'm not sure it isn't true. I'm not sure if a mental relation with a woman doesn't make it impossible to love her. To know the *mind* of a woman is to end in hating her. Love means the pre-cognitive flow—neither strictly has a mind—It is the honest state before the apple.[1]

He provides, for the puritan temperament, a handbook for sinners. In *Women in Love*, for example, the characters of Gerald Crich and Gudrun are the more terrible for representing to him the forcibly controlled desires of his own psyche. There lies between them, as he puts it, an "obscene recognition," and he flies from it into synthetic yogic philosophies and cultural primitivism. It is a flight from the mother in the mind to the father in the blood.

Lawrence Durrell, in his novel *Balthazar*, has one of his characters describe Lawrence as a man with a "habit of building a Taj Mahal around anything as simple as a good f--k." [2] Nothing could be further from the truth. The same unconscious processes we have described in other contexts manifest themselves here as well.

The sexual descriptions in Lawrence's novels contain always the imagery of what is recognizable as coitus anxiety, which implies a neurotic regression to some prior state, before the genitals have assumed primacy as the sexual organ par excellence, when for the child the pleasurable organ is the mouth, which does not give but receives

---

From **Oedipus in Nottingham: D. H. Lawrence** by *Daniel A. Weiss* (Seattle: University of Washington Press, *1963*), *pp.100-101, 102-4.* Copyright © *1963* by University of Washington Press. Reprinted by permission of the publisher.

[1] Huxley, *The Letters of D. H. Lawrence,* p. 688.
[2] Lawrence Durrell, *Balthazar* (New York: E. P. Dutton and Co., 1958) p. 114.

through suckling. The orally dependent infant, for whom all orifices in phantasy satisfy oral (sucking) needs, fears the giving of himself in an orgasm. His own hunger, which he attributes as well to the object of his desire, the nursing mother, threatens to devour him. The neurotic Oedipal man, for whom the nursing situation was the paradisal one, equates orgasm with loss and withdraws in horror from a mother image that is more predator than nurse. The clinical descriptions are consistently those of death; violent, explosive annihilation; and mutilation.[3]

* * *

Women in Love presents ostensibly two men and two women whose relationships are respectively desirable and undesirable. Gerald Crich, the blond man of power, was conceived of by Lawrence as a composite figure, derived from a mine operator in the Midlands coal regions and Lawrence's friend Middleton Murry. Gudrun, Gerald's mistress, is Katherine Mansfield.[4] The character of Rupert Birkin is presumably Lawrence himself. But if we accept this separation of identities we deny the continuity of Lawrence's self-description, and his ubiquity in sexual relationships whose common denominator is the anxiety manifested above. From Birkin's own actions we suspect that his search for "polarity" and "otherness" and the "ultraphallic" emerges from the fear of the intrauterine absorption that his friend Gerald seeks. On the strength of Gerald's actions and his resemblance to other earlier characters in Lawrence's work (the Prussian officer comes to mind), I would maintain that Gerald is psychically closer to Lawrence than Birkin—that Gerald is Lawrence's practical involvement in the world, and Birkin merely, perhaps totally, his dialectic personified.

Gerald Crich, like Paul Morel, comes to a woman for relief, Paul after his mother's death, the other after his father's. Gerald's experience is a curious mixture:

> And she [Gudrun], she was the great bath of life, he worshipped her. Mother and substance of all life she was. And he, child and man, received of her and was made whole. His pure body was almost killed, but the miraculous soft effluence of her breast suffused over him, over his seared, damaged brain, like a healing lymph, like a soft, soothing flow of life itself, perfect as if he were bathed in the womb again. . . . Like a child at the breast he cleaved intensely to her and she could not put him away.[5]

[3] Sylvan Keiser, "Body Ego during Orgasm," *Psychoanalytic Quarterly*, XXI (April, 1952), 153–56 *passim*.
[4] Nehls, *A Composite Biography of D.H. Lawrence*, I, 377.
[5] D. H. Lawrence, *Women in Love* (New York: Modern Library, n.d.), p. 394.

It is between Gerald and Gudrun that the obscene mental recognition of their mutual sensuality occurs, the "shame" that with Will Brangwen "was part of extreme delight." And now in this extravagant image the coitus is transformed into a nursing phantasy in which the brain, in an exotic displacement of orgastic relief, is put to sleep at the breast of the mother, the man becomes infant.

In *Aaron's Rod,* Aaron Sisson, one of Lawrence's composite selves, is sick unto death for having surrendered himself to a woman. " 'I felt it—I felt it go, inside me, the minute I gave in to her. It's perhaps killed me,' " he tells his friend Lilly.[6] Lawrence's women destroy with the power of love. They draw men to them, only to destroy them. In *Aaron's Rod* they are not beaked predators; they are constrictors.

Josephine Hay, the *belle dame* of Aaron's delirium, is an undeveloped version of the Gudrun of *Women in Love.* She is the artist woman, sexually attractive and intellectually aware. She does not fulfill herself sexually at the man's expense but is herself sexually disinherited, Lilith, not Eve. Lawrence envelops her in serpent imagery, describes her licking her "rather full, dry lips with the rapid tip of her tongue. It was an odd movement, suggesting a snake's flicker." [7]

[6] D. H. Lawrence, *Aaron's Rod* (New York: Thomas Seltzer, 1922), p. 95.
[7] *Ibid.,* p. 31.

Chronology of Important Dates

Lawrence's Life	General Events
1885 D. H. Lawrence born September 11 at Eastwood, Nottinghamshire.	
	1890 Frazer, *The Golden Bough*.
	1896 Hardy, *Jude the Obscure*.
	1899–1902 Boer War.
	1900 Conrad, *Lord Jim*. Freud, *The Interpretation of Dreams*.
	1901 Death of Queen Victoria.
1903 Becomes pupil-teacher at Ilkeston, Derbyshire.	
	1905 Einstein's theory of relativity.
1906 Enters Nottingham University.	
1908 Becomes teacher at elementary school in Croydon, Surrey.	
1909 Poems published in *The English Review*.	1909 Pound, *Personae*.
1910 Mother dies in December.	1910–13 Russell and Whitehead, *Principia Mathematica*.
1911 *The White Peacock*.	
1912 Quits teaching job in March. Runs off with Frieda Weekley in April, settles in Italy. *The Trespasser*.	

1913	Sons and Lovers.	1913–27	Proust, *A la recherche du temps perdu.*
1914	Marries in London. Remains in England through the war. *The Prussian Officer* (short stories).	1914–18	First World War.
1915	*The Rainbow* (published September, suppressed in November). "The Crown" ("my philosophy").		
1917	Expelled from Cornwall in October. *Look! We Have Come Through!* (poems).		
		1918	Strachey, *Eminent Victorians.*
1919	Returns to Italy.		
1920	*Women in Love. The Lost Girl.*		
1922	*Aaron's Rod. England, My England* (short stories). Travels to Ceylon, Australia, New Mexico.	1922	Eliot, *The Waste Land.* Joyce, *Ulysses.*
1924	Receives ranch in Taos, New Mexico. Visits Mexico.		
		1925	Gide, *The Counterfeiters.*
1926	*The Plumed Serpent.* Settles in Italy.		
		1927	Woolf, *To the Lighthouse.*
1928	*Lady Chatterley's Lover. Collected Poems.* Leaves Italy for Switzerland and France.	1929	Hemingway, *A Farewell to Arms.* Stock market crash in September.
1930	Dies March 2 at Vence, France.		

Notes on the Editor and Contributors

STEPHEN J. MIKO, editor of this volume, teaches English at the University of California at Santa Barbara. He is working on a book on Lawrence's novels.

GEORGE H. FORD is Chairman of the English Department at the University of Rochester. He is author of *Dickens and His Readers, Keats and the Victorians,* and an editor of the *Norton Anthology of English Literature.*

ALAN FRIEDMAN teaches English at Swarthmore College. He is author of *The Turn of the Novel,* and he is currently writing a novel.

DAVID J. GORDON teaches English at Hunter College. He is author of *D. H. Lawrence as a Literary Critic.*

ROBERT B. HEILMAN is Chairman of the English Department at the University of Washington. His most recent book is *Tragedy and Melodrama.*

EDWIN HONIG teaches English at Brown University. Critic, poet, and translator, he is author of *The Gazebos.*

JULIAN MOYNAHAN is both a critic and novelist, author of *Sisters and Brothers.* He teaches at Rutgers University.

MARK SPILKA teaches English at Brown University. He is author of *Dickens and Kafka: A Mutual Interpretation,* and he is editor of *D. H. Lawrence: A Collection of Critical Essays.*

DANIEL A. WEISS teaches English at the University of Washington and specializes in psychoanalytic criticism.

LEONE VIVANTE is an aesthetician and philosopher, author of *English Poetry and its Contribution to the Knowledge of a Creative Principle.*

ELISEO VIVAS is John Evans Professor of Moral and Intellectual Philosophy at Northwestern University. Among his books are *The Problems of Aesthetics* and *Creation and Discovery.*

Selected Bibliography

There now exists such a large body of criticism and biography on Lawrence that the following selections must be rather arbitrary.

Biography

The most important work is that of Edward Nehls and Harry Moore. Nehls' *D. H. Lawrence: A Composite Biography*, 3 Vols. (Madison: University of Wisconsin Press, 1957-59) assembles passages from Lawrence's works, books about him, and accounts by his friends and acquaintances to make a continuous and fascinating narrative. Harry Moore's two biographies, *The Life and Works of D. H. Lawrence* (New York: Twayne, 1951) and *The Intelligent Heart* (New York: Farrar, Strauss & Giroux, Inc., 1954), provide the most thorough accounts of Lawrence's life.

Criticism

As references in the essays collected here imply, F. R. Leavis' *D. H. Lawrence: Novelist* (New York: Alfred A. Knopf, Inc., 1956) remains one of the most important books on Lawrence's novels. It contains a long and important analysis of *Women in Love*. Before Leavis' work very little first-rate criticism of Lawrence existed. A notable exception, however, is Stephen Potter's *D. H. Lawrence: A First Study* (London: Jonathan Cape Limited, 1930), which concisely and perceptively explores *Woman in Love*'s importance in Lawrence's developing career. Some recent and useful essays follow.

Angelo Bertocci, "Symbolism in *Women in Love*," in Harry T. Moore, ed., *A D. H. Lawrence Miscellany* (Carbondale: Southern Illinois University Press, 1959), pp. 83-102. A symbolist reading emphasizing Lawrence's "romanticism."

Robert L. Chamberlain, "Pussum, Minette, and the Afro-Nordic Symbol in Lawrence's *Women in Love*," *PMLA*, LXXVII (1963), 407-16. Explores color symbolism in relation to changes in various texts of the novel, emphasizes the identity of the African and Nordic themes.

George H. Ford, "An Introductory Note to D. H. Lawrence's Prologue to *Women in Love*," *Texas Quarterly*, VI (1963), 92–98. This prologue is a rejected first chapter, printed here for the first time (pp. 20–39), dealing with the physical relationship between Gerald and Birkin. Ford's remarks help to clarify Lawrence's methods of composition and selection, the prologue itself is explicit about matters glossed over or avoided in the novel as pubished. See Ford above, p. 36.

W. R. Martin, " 'Freedom Together' in D. H. Lawrence's *Women in Love*," *English Studies in Africa*, VIII (1965), 112–20. Pursues Birkin's ideal by contrast with Gerald and Loerke; keeps very close to the text.

Mark Schorer, "*Women in Love* and Death," in Mark Spilka, ed., *D. H. Lawrence: A Collection of Critical Essays* (Englewood Cliffs: Prentice-Hall, Inc., 1963), pp. 50–61. Discusses Lawrence's novel as "psychic drama," relates Lawrence's moral purpose to both style and structure.

TWENTIETH CENTURY
INTERPRETATIONS

MAYNARD MACK, *Series Editor*
Yale University

NOW AVAILABLE
Collections of Critical Essays
ON

ADVENTURES OF HUCKLEBERRY FINN
ALL FOR LOVE
THE AMBASSADORS
ARROWSMITH
AS YOU LIKE IT
BLEAK HOUSE
THE BOOK OF JOB
THE CASTLE
DOCTOR FAUSTUS
DON JUAN
DUBLINERS
THE DUCHESS OF MALFI
ENDGAME
EURIPIDES' ALCESTIS
THE FALL OF THE HOUSE OF USHER
THE FROGS
GRAY'S ELEGY
THE GREAT GATSBY
GULLIVER'S TRAVELS
HAMLET
HARD TIMES

(continued on next page)

(continued from previous page)

HENRY IV, PART TWO
HENRY V
THE ICEMAN COMETH
JULIUS CAESAR
KEATS'S ODES
LIGHT IN AUGUST
LORD JIM
MUCH ADO ABOUT NOTHING
THE NIGGER OF THE "NARCISSUS"
OEDIPUS REX
THE OLD MAN AND THE SEA
PAMELA
THE PLAYBOY OF THE WESTERN WORLD
THE PORTRAIT OF A LADY
A PORTRAIT OF THE ARTIST AS A YOUNG MAN
THE PRAISE OF FOLLY
PRIDE AND PREJUDICE
THE RAPE OF THE LOCK
THE RIME OF THE ANCIENT MARINER
ROBINSON CRUSOE
SAMSON AGONISTES
THE SCARLET LETTER
SIR GAWAIN AND THE GREEN KNIGHT
SONGS OF INNOCENCE AND OF EXPERIENCE
THE SOUND AND THE FURY
THE TEMPEST
TESS OF THE D'URBERVILLES
TOM JONES
TWELFTH NIGHT
UTOPIA
VANITY FAIR
WALDEN
THE WASTE LAND
WOMEN IN LOVE
WUTHERING HEIGHTS